THE NEGRO

WHAT NEGROES WANT; WHY AND HOW THEY
ARE FIGHTING; WHOM THEY SUPPORT; WHAT
WHITES THINK OF THEM AND THEIR DEMANDS

BASED ON THE NATIONWIDE SURVEY BY *Newsweek* MAGAZINE

REVOLUTION

IN AMERICA

WILLIAM BRINK • LOUIS HARRIS

A CLARION BOOK
PUBLISHED BY SIMON AND SCHUSTER

A CLARION BOOK
PUBLISHED BY SIMON AND SCHUSTER
ROCKEFELLER CENTER, 630 FIFTH AVENUE
NEW YORK, NEW YORK 10020
ALL RIGHTS RESERVED
INCLUDING THE RIGHT OF REPRODUCTION
IN WHOLE OR IN PART IN ANY FORM
COPYRIGHT © 1963 BY NEWSWEEK, INC.

SECOND PAPERBACK PRINTING

SBN 671-20419-X
LIBRARY OF CONGRESS CATALOG CARD NUMBER: 64-13340
MANUFACTURED IN THE UNITED STATES OF AMERICA

. . . dedicated
to the proposition
that all men are created equal. . . .

ACKNOWLEDGMENTS

IN ANY UNDERTAKING as massive as the Negro and white studies which form the basis of this book, many hands obviously were involved, from the initial interviews all over the country down to the checking of the last statistic.

The authors wish to pay tribute to the loyal staff of Louis Harris and Associates, without whose tireless efforts this analysis of Negro and white attitudes and opinions would never have been possible. In particular they are indebted to Tom Stanton, Florence Weinsoff, Richard Stryker, Fred McOmber, Barbara Enders, Paul Funkhouser, Ruth Clark, Helen Bowlen, Ralph Brown, Lawrence Houppert and the patient, hard-working and creative people interviewing in the field, coding the volunteered responses, and tabulating the results. As a team, these people performed literal miracles in telescoping time, without compromising quality or accuracy.

In the compilation of their material, the authors leaned heavily on *Newsweek*'s domestic bureaus, whose skilled and enthusiastic staffers not only helped with the interviewing but contributed much other indispensable information. While all deserve credit, special thanks go to Joseph Cumming and Karl Fleming of the Atlanta Bureau for their invaluable advice and counsel, and to Patricia Reilly, Janet Smith, Carol Dimmit, Nancy Mintz and Constance Montague of *Newsweek*'s Research Staff, who labored long and selfless hours to ensure the accuracy of each statement made in the book.

A very special debt of gratitude is owed Elizabeth Sutherland of Simon and Schuster for her constant encouragement, her perceptive editing and her indefatigable help in getting the book to press.

Finally, no acknowledgment could possibly be complete without mention of Osborn Elliott, Editor of *Newsweek*, who can truthfully be called the "father" of the entire project. It was Mr. Elliott who first perceived the great lack of accurate information about Negro and white attitudes and who directed that these *Newsweek* polls be made. His was the foresight and courage that produced the *Newsweek* cover stories in July and October 1963, his the inspiration that led to the writing of this book. And it was his final editing of the manuscript that, more than anything else, made *The Negro Revolution in America* a reality. In fact, this very acknowledgment was the only part of the book out of bounds for Mr. Elliott's sharp editor's pencil. He would have cut it.

WILLIAM BRINK
LOUIS HARRIS

New York
October 1963

CONTENTS

PREFACE

BY OSBORN ELLIOTT
Editor, *Newsweek*

JOURNALISM is a rewarding profession for the simple reason that it involves the pursuit of truth. Daily the journalist is challenged to identify the false, to sift the big truths from the small and to bring a sense of order to events as they hurtle pell-mell into history. But journalism can be frustrating as well, for the truth is an elusive quarry. Any cub reporter with two versions of an automobile accident can testify to that. So can any correspondent who has covered a summit conference, or a political convention, or a war. And when it is a matter of determining the deepest emotions and aspirations of a people, who is to say where the truth really lies?

Perhaps the most remarkable aspect of one of the biggest news stories of 1963 was that so few facts about it were known. Everywhere in the United States the Negro was on the march, demanding equality. The surface evidence is plain for all to see and hear—on every front page, on every television screen and radio—as the bombs burst in Birmingham and the song of revolution rang out across the land: "We Shall Overcome." But what lay behind the movement, and why had it suddenly gained such momentum? Why 1963? What, precisely, did the Negroes want, and in what order? What did they mean by "freedom"? How far were they willing to go to achieve their goals? What did they think of the white man? Not even Negro leaders could say for sure—indeed, no one could say how Negroes rated their own leaders or even who the leaders were. Not only were Negroes themselves unsure of the facts; there was a deep and dangerous void between whites and Negroes in America, a no man's land of ignorance.

So it was, in mid-1963, that the editors of *Newsweek* decided to search out the truth about this remarkable social revolution. Normal journalistic methods, we concluded, were inadequate to the job of probing 19 million hearts. Accordingly, we decided on a marriage between the art of journalism and the new science of public-opinion analysis. We chose as our partners Louis Harris and Associates—a man and an organization that had long since won the respect of professional politicians for accurately determining voting trends and attitudes in election after election, from coast to coast. By combining Harris' scientific methods of statistical research and the journalist's talent for converting numbers into meaningful words, we felt that we could develop the kind of information needed by a democratic society seeking solutions to its most pressing problem.

The first job—and, as it turned out, one of the hardest—was to select a cross-section of American Negroes who would accurately represent the whole—by age, income, location, occupation, sex, etc. This task was made difficult by the fact that Congress has forbidden the Census Bureau to provide detailed breakdowns on Negro population, block by block. For many other ethnic groups such information is available—but not in the case of nonwhites. This is so for a curious reason. On the one hand, a number of racist politicians from the South believe that by making such a breakdown, Census would lend too much identity to the Negroes; on the other, a number of liberals from the North believe that it would tend even more to segregate Negroes as a race apart.

The Federal government does, however, provide figures on Negro population for larger geographic units—counties and major urban divisions—and this information provided the general areas to be sampled: about 60 population clusters in all. As the selection process began, every Negro in the country over the age of 18 had an equal chance to be selected for interviewing. Harris field workers then fanned out into the 60 areas for on-the-spot surveys. They talked to local officials, pounded the pavements, rang doorbells and came back with mapped estimates of Negro population concentration within sections of cities, towns and rural areas. These concentration points were then listed according to the size of their Negro population. The next breakdown was into blocks—again at random, proportionate to size. From the blocks selected, particular households were chosen on the same basis. Within each household every family member was then listed, and finally the individual to be interviewed was selected on the spot in a random draw among the members of the household, with certain controls to guarantee a proper range of sex and ages among those interviewed. More than 1,000 Negroes were thus chosen.

While all this was going on, many hours were spent compiling a questionnaire calculated to draw from people their innermost thoughts and feelings on certain crucial issues. The questionnaire grew to 252 questions, many of them designed to touch the nerve ends of the Negro psyche. Some of the questions required simple yes-or-no answers; others were "open-ended," designed to encourage respondents to answer at length. The questionnaire was tested in a number of trial interviews. Certain revisions were made, and it was decided to use Negro interviewers wherever possible, in the belief that they were more likely to get Negroes talking honestly and at length about themselves. In the end, 158 interviewers were selected—all but six of them Negroes. Most of the interviewers were teachers, principals or graduate students; several were clergymen. Before going out on the job, each interviewer was asked to answer the questionnaire himself, in order to screen out any whose personal attitudes might distort the poll's results.

To bolster the Harris organization in this massive project, *Newsweek* appointed a task force of 40 reporters, writers and researchers under the direction of Washington Bureau Chief

Benjamin Bradlee. This team, in consultation with Negroes in a number of cities, picked a list of 100 Negro leaders (see page 243). The leaders were not merely front-page names; they included a number of lesser known but influential businessmen, ministers, doctors, etc. Each was interviewed with the same questionnaire, so that the leaders' views could be compared with those of the rank and file.

As a steaming heat wave hung over the nation in July, the Harris and *Newsweek* interviewers set out for the chosen sample areas—the South Side of Chicago; Riviera Beach, Florida; French's Creek, North Carolina; Baltimore, Philadelphia, New York, Dallas and half a hundred other places. In a few days reports from the field indicated that our technique was working well; the interviews were averaging two and a quarter hours apiece, and the first results showed that we were on the way to developing history's most comprehensive X-ray of the mind and heart of the Negro in America.

Newsmen are supposed to be thick-skinned and not easily moved by what they encounter. But as this project progressed, a sense of excitement seized each and every one involved. For most of us this was the discovery of another world, as strange as the other side of the moon—the dark side. We will not soon forget the things we saw, the people we met:

. . . The Negro police captain in Chicago, quietly but sharply issuing orders to white policemen who obviously respected their commander. The *Newsweek* correspondent who interviewed the captain used to cover that precinct as a police reporter. "Ten years ago," he recalled, "that neighborhood was white and the very idea of a Negro police captain was beyond anyone's comprehension. The word 'nigger' used to be part of the language in that station. I had a feeling we'd come a long way."

. . . The sharecropper in South Carolina, scratching out a bare subsistence from the hostile red-clay soil, dreaming of a few acres of his own—but knowing that it was only a dream. "If I don't make it here," he told his interviewer, "I don't make it."

. . . The time a gang of teen-agers began to hoot and heckle a Harris worker as she was finishing her last interview in a Southern town. The cop on the beat came up and asked her what she was doing, then advised her to get out of town.

. . . The interview with comedian Dick Gregory, conducted from 9 P.M. to 2:20 A.M., between shows at San Francisco's hungry i night club. Thoughtful and articulate, Gregory shunted off well-wishers after each show to get back into the manager's stuffy office to continue the interview. At one point Gregory could not resist a gag: "There may not be much difference between whites and Negroes, but you guys have the missiles."

Every night the questionnaires were airmailed back to New York, where the results were coded, transcribed onto IBM cards, converted to magnetic tape and fed into the giant 7090 computer. This machine tallied up the statistical results of 3,000 man-hours of interviewing in 18 minutes. But machines cannot measure emotions; this job was left to the *Newsweek* team in New York, who plowed through the 1,257 completed questionnaires and from them extracted 3,000 quotes for possible use.

The writing fell to Washington Bureau Chief Ben Bradlee and five others: William Brink (co-author of this volume), then Chicago Bureau Chief, Peter Goldman, Jonathan Rinehart, James M. Cannon and Peter Andrews. The result was an 18-page special section in the July 29, 1963, issue of *Newsweek*, which was to draw a gratifying amount of praise from many directions, from whites and Negroes alike. Just as their own hearts had been touched by their experiences, the people who worked on this project seemed able to communicate their feelings to others. The 13-year-old son of one correspondent read the issue with great interest. When he learned that his father had contributed the profile of an Atlanta postal worker, he said, "I just feel like I want to call that man up and talk to him."

While the reaction to our survey was enthusiastic, we realized that only half the job had been done. Clearly, the facts about the Negro and his demands were vital—but how did the white man feel about this new social revolution and the people behind it? How much equality was the white man willing to see the Negro get? How broad and deep did white prejudice against the Negro really run? On the answers to these questions—no less than on Negro demands—would depend the course of race relations in America for years to come.

Once again, in September, the Harris organization went to work, compiling a new questionnaire aimed at whites; once again, interviewers moved into the field; once again, the extended-interview technique succeeded in getting deep beneath the surface of man's intellect and emotions. One man in a small Pennsylvania town wrote that he was so disturbed by the interview that he couldn't sleep. He had thought long and hard about his answers, which were mildly prejudiced, and had talked about them with his wife and his minister. He did not want to be quoted by name, he said, since his answers had not accurately reflected his true (or new) views on the subject.

More than 1,200 white people were interviewed by the survey. The results appeared as a special section written by James M. Cannon and Mel Elfin and edited by Lester Bernstein in the October 21, 1963, issue of *Newsweek*. Some of the findings were hopeful, but, as Chapter 9 of this book makes all too clear, the profile of prejudice that emerged was unpleasant to read. Some of the women who originally transcribed the results onto IBM cards were Negroes. Midway through their chore it appeared that they might walk off the job; they thought, from the ugly bias of many statements, that they were working for some racist cause. Only when told the nature of the survey did they agree to continue their work.

It is a cliché in journalism for a reporter to say he has enough information on a story to write a book. But in this instance it was literally true. Not only did we have more information than we could possibly use in a weekly news magazine; it seemed to us that the nature of our information was so unique, and so important, that it should be made available in lasting form for the readers of today and the historians of tomorrow. Accordingly, co-authors William Brink and Louis Harris set to work, going back to the original survey material and doing long hours of additional research on everything from slavery to Freedom Rides, from Supreme Court decisions to the role of the Negro church in America. They reinterviewed some of the leaders, greatly expanded the original report and added much that is new. Scattered through the book the reader will find a number of abbreviated statistical tables; in the Appendix, these tables and many more are treated in full.

The editors of *Newsweek* are proud to have been associated with this undertaking from the beginning; for myself, no journalistic experience has been more stimulating. The story behind the present volume has been a dramatic and deeply human one from start to finish. For on the very day this book was to go to press in final form—November 22, 1963—President John F. Kennedy was assassinated in Dallas, Texas. The total effect of that shattering event on the course of the Negro revolution is for future books to record. The revolution continues, with a long future and many unpredictable factors.

But the quest for truth goes on. And in this case, the quest is far more than a journalistic concern. An entire people is caught up in it, searching to discover how to give substance to the truths we supposedly hold self-evident.

O. E.

CHAPTER **1**

A RACE
AWAKENED

THERE ARE TIMES in human history when deep currents of change run unnoticed for years before they boil, turbulent and insistent, to the surface. So it was, for example, with the tide of nationalism that arose among the colonial peoples of Asia and Africa after World War II. And so it has been with the revolution of the Negro in contemporary America.

For more than two hundred years the Negroes of the United States had been chained—first by slavery and then by segregation and discrimination. On the whole they seemed passive and content with their lot. But this was not really so, for no race can accept forever the proposition that it is inferior to another. From half-hidden depths of impatience and anger the Negro revolution began rising to a crescendo of protest in the middle of the twentieth century. During the 1950s there were sporadic incidents, a handful of Negro children here

19

and there seeking entrance to white schools in the South. There were ugly and ominous trouble spots, such as Little Rock. But as yet the real proportions of the Negro's revolt were not clearly visible. Then came more and more incidents—Freedom Riders demanding equal treatment at bus terminals and sit-in demonstrators asking for service at lunch counters. Even so, many said that such protests were the work of a few rabble-rousing troublemakers. Then in 1963 came Birmingham, with its police dogs and fire hoses turned on the Negro marchers; Birmingham, with the church bombing that took the lives of four little Negro girls and two boys during its aftermath. Then also came the march of the Negroes to the capital of their country, the most awesome display of a race in protest that the United States had ever seen.

Suddenly it began to dawn on white America that this was a full-fledged social revolution. It was now perfectly plain that the Negroes did not want just a place in a white school or a seat at a white lunch counter. What they wanted was nothing less than the full equality which is supposedly the birthright of every American, white or black. What they proposed was the greatest change in the social fabric of the United States since its very beginning, and a new way of life that few American whites had ever before known. Many whites might not like it; many would actively oppose it. But however they might feel, the whites could not ignore the Negro's demand, for it went straight to the heart of America's hallowed creed of liberty and justice for all. Almost 180 years after the Founding Fathers wrote the U.S. Constitution, white America was being asked, at long last, to live up to that creed.

In any event of such magnitude, many different voices, both white and Negro, are bound to be raised and many gradations of opinion expressed. In the South, Governor George Wallace of Alabama seemed to epitomize the hard-shell resistance of that troubled area when he cried: "I draw the line in the dust and toss the gauntlet before the feet of tyranny, and I say segregation now, segregation tomorrow, segregation forever." But Harry Ashmore, who was the temperate editor of *The*

Arkansas Gazette during the Little Rock crisis, has said that integration is not "socially or morally wrong; I think in time all the barriers will be down. . . ."

On the Negro side, the Rev. Joseph H. Jackson, head of the National Baptist Convention, counseled caution lest the Negroes "become so anxious to win an immediate victory for the race that we make secondary the winning of spiritual victory for the nation. . . ." But, the Rev. Martin Luther King, Jr., cried: "We're through with tokenism and gradualism and see-how-far-you've-comeism. . . . We can't wait any longer. Now is the time."

In the *Newsweek* poll of white people, their contrasting views on the subject of the Negro's fight for equality came through clearly. In Virginia City, Nevada, Richard J. Lunetta, a 34-year-old design engineer, said this: "I feel equal rights is wrong politically, morally and socially. Man was just not born to be equal in all ways. . . . In fact, in my opinion, there is no such thing as equal rights, or 'all men are created equal,' because history and society just aren't built that way." But Robert Rathbone, who owns a construction business in Vestal, New York, took the opposite tack: "I don't think that they [the Negroes] are asking for too much. They only expect the same rights that we have. They only want the same chances we have for a better life."

Among the whites, Rathbone's comment came as close as any to recognizing the true nature of the Negro revolution. Over and over again in the interviews, that is what the Negroes themselves said they wanted. As Dr. Byron Biscoe, a Negro dentist in Oklahoma City, Oklahoma, put it: "I'd like to see the Negro change from a second-class citizen to a first-class citizen. That takes in everything we're fighting for—all our rights. How do you explain to a child that he can't take a 25-cent pony ride because of the pigment of his skin, or that he can't sit in front and watch the bus driver?"

From out of the divergent voices of the white and Negro communities, one fact became clear: There is a huge gulf between the two peoples, a yawning absence of communication and ordinary human contact. To a great many white Americans, the Negro is a mystery almost as dark as his skin. If the average white thinks of the Negro at all, he is likely to think of him as the man who shines his shoes, who mows his lawn, washes his car, delivers his mail, sings or dances on TV, or plays first base at the ball park. Once the Negro has finished with these pursuits, it seems, he vanishes somewhere into a remote and shadowy world of his own.

The truth, of course, is that not many white Americans have ever bothered to take a close look at the world of the Negro. Mostly it is a world of poverty. In the shimmering, bright-leafed tobacco lands of eastern North Carolina or the black, alluvial cotton fields of the Mississippi Delta, it is a world of share-croppers living in unpainted clapboard shacks. These dwellings have a drab sameness, with their sagging chimneys and rusty tin roofs. Almost always there is a patch of collard greens in the yard and, for a brave touch of the niceties of life, an array of glass jars and coffee cans filled with geraniums and petunias on the porch. Very likely there is an old car waiting on wooden blocks for the day when its owner can afford to put it back in shape. A chopping block and a rusty ax stand beside a pile of logs to feed the wood stove inside. As often as not, a lop-sided, unpainted outhouse is sitting back in the weeds.

Poverty has a different face in the great Negro slums of the North. There, in a ceaseless din of automobiles, jukeboxes and whooping, ragged children, the Negro is likely to live in a rotting tenement, its doors scarred with carved initials, its broken windows stuffed with rags and newspapers and its interior infested with cockroaches and rats.

Negro ghettos tend to acquire names. They may be Little Harlem, named for one of the worst of them all in New York, or Baptist Town, or Bronzeville, or Catfish Row, or perhaps just plain Nigger Town. Yet not all Negroes live in them. Collier Heights, in Atlanta, Georgia, is dotted with Negro homes costing $25,000 to $50,000—surrounded by gracious lawns, equipped with back-yard grills and even, here and there, swimming pools. Almost any large city has a similar section where the better-off Negroes dwell. And, of course, there are thousands upon thousands of Negroes who live middle-class lives not very different from that of the average white—except for the great gulf of color.

By the same token, not many Negroes have any real idea of what it means to be a part of white society. Because of the segregation and discrimination that have shackled their lives, they rarely know the freedom of being able to select the restaurant or hotel of their choice without the slightest thought that they might be turned away. They do not know what it means, in most cases, to be able to buy their "dream home," to send their children to the school they desire, or to apply for the job they really want. The Negroes, however, have long seen and envied the advantages of white society, and one of the clearest purposes of their revolution now is to share in those advantages.

Although his struggle for equal rights has been essentially nonviolent, the Negro has had his battlegrounds. In the history books of the future, Little Rock, Montgomery, Oxford and Birmingham may have the same ring as Vicksburg, Antietam, Gettysburg and Shiloh, of the Civil War. He has had his heroes —in the militant leaders who have gone out to direct his cause, in the hordes of followers who have demonstrated and gone to jail, in the hundreds of Negro children who have braved the curses and spittle of whites so as to enter newly integrated schools. The Negro has had his martyrs—in Medgar Evers, the NAACP worker who was slain in Mississippi, and in the six youngsters killed in the Birmingham bombing. Yet all of the Negro's effort had, by the early 1960s, brought him only grudging and piecemeal concessions. In their hearts, the *Newsweek* poll of whites showed, most white people know that the cause of the Negro is just. But, out of attitudes hardened over hundreds of years, they are loath to take the great and final step of admitting him to an equal place in all parts of their society. Whites are bitter because there no longer seems to be any other way out. Always before they have been able to find some way to contain the Negro—by giving him his own school or confining him to a ghetto so that he didn't get too close. But the day of accommodation is fast disappearing. The insistent demands of the Negroes are invading every segment of society. They have affected the schools, the courts and the churches; businessmen, builders and city planners; local and Federal government. Each white is now obliged to look at the Negro's revolution and assess what should be done about it.

Where will the revolution go? One clear answer is that it won't stop. The Negroes could not now cease their drive for civil rights even if they wanted to, which they do not. More than that, the problem they pose can only get bigger, if for no other reason than that the Negroes themselves are becoming more numerous. At present, Negroes comprise about 10 per cent of the U.S. population, but their population is growing at a faster rate than that of the whites. In the decade of 1960–70, a total of 40 million births is expected. Six million of these will be Negro, which is better than 10 per cent. Also by 1970 there will be 18 million Negroes living in the cities (vs. 13.8 million in 1960), a figure which is nearly twice the population of the six New England states and greater than the entire population of Canada. By 1975 Negroes are expected to outnumber whites within the corporate city limits of Chicago, as they already do in Washington, D.C. Much the same sort of trend toward heavy Negro populations is taking place in other major cities of the North. All this adds up to more and more demands from the Negroes—for housing and jobs, for political representation. Indeed, the political implications of the Negro revolution have already caused Presidents Kennedy and Johnson to take a stronger stand for civil-rights legislation and have opened a widening rift between the liberal and conservative forces of the Republican Party. In the 1964 Presidential election, the Negro revolution is certain to figure heavily, as it no doubt will in future elections.

What their revolt might ultimately avail the Negroes—and when—are more difficult questions to answer. Even if they were suddenly to be granted first-class citizenship, not all of the problems of the Negroes would be solved. In the South they would still face resistance not only from diehard white supremacists but also from many Southern whites who believe in a segregated way of life simply because they have never known anything else. In the cities it would take many years and untold billions of dollars to move the Negroes out of the ghettos and into decent housing. And even if employers were prepared to give the Negroes better jobs, as many of them increasingly are, many Negroes would not be qualified for them until they had more education and job training.

Moreover, Negro leaders themselves are aware that some white criticisms of Negroes are true. Their crime rate is too high—although statistics vary on this point and authorities have pointed out that correction of Negroes is easier and false arrests more frequent than among whites. According to a 1962 report of the FBI, Negroes account for 30 per cent of all crimes while constituting 10 per cent of the population. Their record was a good deal worse when it came to certain types of crime, including the most violent: 57 per cent of robberies, 60 per cent of murders and non-negligent manslaughters. The rate of illegitimate births in the Negro population was vastly higher than in the white population. Statistics provided by the National Urban League indicate that in 1962–63 one in every five nonwhite births was illegitimate, compared with one in every fifty white births. The Negroes also have been greatly dependent on public welfare. In 1958 more than two-fifths of all families receiving aid for dependent children were nonwhite.

Negroes (and white sociologists) point out, of course, that these things are produced by the vicious circle that has ruled their lives: if they were not downtrodden they would not resort to crime; if their family structure had not been undermined as far back as slavery they would have more stable marital relations; if they had better job opportunities they would not need relief. But the further point that the Negroes make is that they will never be able to improve all of these conditions unless they are granted equal rights now. Whitney Young of the National Urban League has gone so far as to suggest that Negroes be given, at least at the beginning, better than an even break. "What we need," Young told *Newsweek,* "is a massive domestic Marshall Plan that for a period will give special, preferential and expanded opportunities for Negro citizens in housing, employment, health, welfare and education —the same conscious effort to *include* which the society historically has exhibited in *exclusion*."

In truth no one can foretell with any degree of accuracy what the future of the Negro revolution will be. Conceivably it could drag on for many years, with the same kind of slow, agonizing attrition that has marked its progress until now. This is probably what many whites hope for and what Negro leaders dread, for they are aware that the revolt has drained a great deal of energy and money from their people and that their resolve might well flag in a prolonged struggle. At worst the revolution could develop such bitterness as to throw the races, white and black, into virtual armed camps. At best the whites may themselves decide sooner than expected to cast out prejudice and install the Negroes in their rightful place.

But whatever turn the Negro revolution takes, it bears one unmistakable stamp, and that is seemingly unquenchable hope. Throughout the *Newsweek* poll, the Negroes who were interviewed expressed an abiding optimism about the future and an abiding faith in the human decency of whites. The Negroes were sure that within the white population there are many who, while they might not feel free as yet to speak out, would eventually be counted on their side. And as evidence they pointed to the thousands of whites who took part in their grand march to Washington in August 28, 1963.

It was also in Washington that the Rev. Martin Luther King, Jr., the symbolic leader of the revolution, summed up all the Negro's aspirations with his moving "I have a dream" speech.

"I have a dream," intoned King, "that one day this nation will rise up and live out the true meaning of its creed: 'We hold these truths to be self-evident, that all men are created equal.'

"I have a dream that my four little children will one day live in a nation where they will not be judged by the color of their skin but by the content of their character.

"I have a dream that one day every valley shall be exalted,

every hill and mountain shall be made low, the rough places will be made plain, and the crooked places will be made straight, and the glory of the Lord shall be revealed and all flesh shall see it together.

"This is our hope."

CHAPTER 2

MYRDAL
REVISITED

IT HAS BEEN a generation since Gunnar Myrdal, the great Swedish economist and sociologist, examined the life and times of the Negro in the United States in his massive work *An American Dilemma.** To Myrdal the American dilemma was the fundamental clash between the abiding faith of white Americans in their creed of liberty and justice for all and the certain knowledge that they were denying this democratic heritage to the Negro. That breach, Myrdal concluded, should and must be closed for the future welfare of the nation, both at home and in its relations with other nations around the globe.

In the mid-1960s it is all too obvious that the American dilemma remains, though not quite on the same terms as Myrdal

* Harper & Row, 1944, 1962. See also *The Negro in America,* an authorized condensation, by Arnold Rose, Harper & Brothers, 1948; Beacon Press, 1956.

28

found it. Twenty years ago America was doing very little—nor cared—to come to grips with its problem. Today, however much white people might wish to continue to ignore it, "the Negro problem" will not go away and leave them alone. They are being pressed more and more by the Negroes themselves to confront it, to weigh it and ultimately, as Myrdal hoped, to do something about it.

Not too long ago there was a popular theory among wishful-thinking whites, and even among some authorities on race relations, that the simple passage of time would somehow solve all the problems of transforming the Negroes from an oppressed and segregated minority into fully equal citizens. Not very many people believe this now—least of all the Negroes themselves. In their view, mere time hasn't solved anything. Some Negroes, the *Newsweek* poll found, tend to think of their search for civil rights in terms of the century that has passed since Abraham Lincoln issued the Emancipation Proclamation in 1863. "We have been waiting one hundred years," they say. But many others go much farther back, to some 450 years ago when the first black man came to the New World with the early explorers. A member of Christopher Columbus' crew is believed by some scholars to have been black, and Negroes are said to have accompanied Balboa and Cortes.

Aside from these early voyagers, the arrival of the Negro in English America is dated by historians at 1619, when a Dutch man-of-war dropped anchor at Jamestown, Virginia, with a load of twenty blacks whom the captain promptly sold into slavery.* It was the beginning of a history which could hardly make America proud.

Even before the discovery of America, slavery was practiced by European countries. The slave trade began in 1444 when a Portuguese prince named Henry the Navigator sent a raiding party to Africa, and over the next 400 years it cost Africa 40 million of its people. In America, the Negro's dark

---

* Lerone Bennet, Jr., in his readable and valuable *Before the Mayflower: A History of the Negro in America, 1619-1962,* notes that this was a year before the celebrated *Mayflower* reached our shores.

skin had much to do with his servitude. The colonies had tried enslaving American Indians, but they tended to sicken and die laboring in the fields. White indentured servants proved more durable, but it was too easy for them to flee and mingle undetected with the general population. It was the Negro whose stamina was equal to the burden of enforced labor and whose dark skin made him readily distinguishable as a slave.

The human degradation, misery and brutality of the slave trade was stupendous. Foraging up and down West Africa, the slave-traders drove their victims—naked and chained by the ankle—like cattle to the coast, where they were examined for defects, branded with hot irons on the chest and clapped into the holds of waiting slave ships. Lerone Bennet reports that some were chained by the neck and leg to shelves no more than 18 inches high for a voyage that would last two or three months. Many went mad and even more died, so that sharks learned to follow the slave ships all the way across the Atlantic to America.

Nor was the Negro's lot very much better here for the next 200 years and more after his arrival. By 1860 there were at least four million Negroes in America. To be sure, a sizable number were free Negroes in the North and the South (close to 500,000 at the middle of the century), but most remained slaves, and the most oppressed were slaves to King Cotton in the South. To keep the plantations going, the slaves were whipped out of their miserable beds and whipped to work in the fields. Family life was torn asunder, with children snatched from their parents and wives or husbands sold away from their mates. The primary motive of the slaveowners was simply to make money from the sale of slaves, but a secondary motive was to prevent the Negroes from forming a stable family life and thus achieve cohesiveness as a race.

Negro men and women were also encouraged to breed like animals, in or out of wedlock, so that the slaveholders would acquire more slaves. Not at all uncommon in those times was the keeping of strong, healthy Negroes as "stud" Negroes and the open advertisement of "breeding slaves." It also became very much the fashion for slaveowners, sports and bachelors

to dally with Negro women, with the result that many Negroes today are of mixed blood. Melville J. Herskovits, in a 1930 study, found that fully 71.7 per cent of the Negroes he surveyed had some white ancestry.* And Louis Lomax has written: "The American Negro is a man—not God—made race." †
In looking back at the slave era, of course, it is important to remember that slavery was legal, and practiced in the best of circles. George Washington and Thomas Jefferson were slaveowners, and so was Patrick Henry.

Scholars may now argue whether the Civil War was really fought over slavery, or the spread of slavery, or something else again. But the net result, as far as the Negro was concerned, appeared to be deliverance from his bondage with the Emancipation Proclamation. He had also on his side the Fourteenth Amendment of 1868, with its due process and equal protection of the laws clause; the Fifteenth Amendment of 1870, which gave all citizens the right to vote regardless of race, color or previous condition of servitude; and the Civil Rights Bill of 1875, which called for "equal enjoyment of the accommodations, advantages, facilities, and privileges of inns, public conveyances on land or water, theaters, and other places of public amusement."

But during the turbulent Reconstruction period of some twenty years after the Civil War, it became clear that the Negro was not going to be free after all. For one thing, after his years of subjugation, illiteracy and landlessness, he was almost totally unprepared to move into a free society. He had no land and therefore no basis on which to build a new society of his own. Cast adrift, thousands of Negroes died of disease and want.

Myrdal wrote that emancipation was not related to any change of mind on the part of white people; it was simply thrust upon the South. And the South began to fight back. While the Ku Klux Klan and other organized bands harried and terrorized the Negro, the Southern states acted to deny him his vote (with literacy and property tests, poll taxes and the infamous

* *The Anthropometry of the American Negro,* Columbia University Press, 1930.
† *The Negro Revolt,* Harper & Row, 1962.

grandfather clause *) and to hobble him with all manner of Jim Crow † laws. Tennessee began these in 1881 with segregated seating in railroad cars, and by the early 1900s there was a vast proliferation of laws segregating the Negro in schools, hospitals, prisons, funeral homes, cemeteries. In Birmingham, Alabama, Lerone Bennet reports, there was even a law forbidding Negroes to play checkers with whites. Meanwhile, the U.S. Supreme Court had, in 1883, found the Civil Rights Bill of 1875 unconstitutional, and in 1896—in the celebrated case of *Plessy* vs. *Ferguson*—it gave its blessing to the wall of segregation the South was building, with its "separate but equal" doctrine. Segregation and its handmaiden, discrimination, thereby became imbedded in the law of the land, not to be seriously challenged for another half-century.

Remarkably, the miserable lot of the Negro in early America did not destroy his loyalty to the country. A runaway slave named Crispus Attucks was the first to fall dead in the Boston Massacre of 1770. Other Negroes fought with distinction in the Revolution and the Civil War and were to do so again later in the great world wars and the Korean War. Yet even if he has shown a sense of identification with America, there is no doubt that slavery and later segregation have made it difficult for the Negro to find a true identity for himself. Torn as he was from his original homeland, and forced to accept new cultural patterns in America, the Negro was denied the chance—enjoyed by European immigrants—to make a proper cultural transition. Bewildered and confused by his treatment in America, the Negro's answer over the years was to try to imitate white America, to adopt what has been called "cultural whiteness." The Negro

* Thus named because this clause in state voting laws allowed persons to vote if their ancestors had voted. Its effect was to disenfranchise Negroes while permitting poor whites—who might also be unable to meet the literacy and property tests—to vote.

† There are a variety of theories as to the origin of this term. According to one of the most prevalent, there was an actual Negro slave named James Crow, whom the poet and songwriter Thomas Dartmouth Rice immortalized as a dialect character in a musical show presented at New York's Bowery Theater in 1832. By 1838 "Jim Crow" had become a familiar synonym for "Negro" with comic overtones. A year later, an antislavery book was published called *The History of Jim Crow*.

of today, sociologists have noted, shows almost no signs of his African heritage except for the color of his skin. Indeed, one of the lessons of the *Newsweek* survey is that the Negro generally rejects the notion that he has any ties with his African homeland. He has spoken the same language as white Americans, worshiped the same God and adhered, ironically, to the same democratic ideals. Myrdal found, in fact, that in emulating the white man the Negro tended to go in for exaggerations of white institutions. When he was not wanted in the white man's church, for example, the Negro founded his own church, a formidable organization often characterized by a fervor unknown to most whites. The great tragedy for the Negro was that, while he obviously hoped by conscious imitation to win acceptance into the white world, his effort availed him almost nothing. In a land noted as a melting pot for many foreign cultures, the Negro has not, at least until now, been allowed to melt.

A major reason for this is rooted in the Jim Crow pattern that emerged after the Civil War, when it became clear that what Southern whites seemed to reject most violently was personal association with the people they had considered, under slavery, to be less than human. They did not want to sit with the Negro or eat with him (though, paradoxically, they would tolerate him as a house servant who prepared their food and cuddled their children). Above all, the whites did not want their women to have intercourse with the Negro or marry him. In his day, Myrdal found that whites saw discrimination in exactly the reverse order from the way Negroes saw it. That is, the whites placed the highest taboo on personal relations, headed by intermarriage, and the least on such matters as jobs for the Negroes. The Negroes, on the other hand, resented discrimination most when it came to jobs and bread, since this is what they needed the most, and least in their personal relations with whites. The *Newsweek* poll substantiated that the Negro puts the emphasis on his physical welfare first and other matters secondarily, and he hardly talks at all about intermarriage. But it is also clear that, by now, he wants at least an equal *right* to do anything he pleases.

Sociologists have detected in the culture pattern of America a curious inertia of the masses, or lack of self-generating movements for almost any kind of cause. Save for the American Revolution itself, there are few examples of any great numbers of Americans rising up to obtain a right or to redress a wrong. Myrdal attributes this "mass passivity," as he calls it, to the growth of America through large infusions of immigrants from many countries, which prevented the development of class solidarity, particularly in the lower classes. The American Negroes presumably have shared this heritage of passivity, and that is why their twentieth-century revolution is so remarkable. Yet it would be a mistake to suppose that only recently have the Negroes taken up their cause of equality, for, in one way or another, they have been struggling against their bonds since the very beginning.

The slave era itself was marked by hundreds of revolts and conspiracies, many of them bloody affairs, in which numerous whites and Negroes were killed. In the South, under the constant threat of swift and terrible punishment, the Negro practiced a servile obeisance to the white man, removing his hat in his presence and sirring him. But he would cheat the white man, if he could, and he had no compunctions about raiding the master's chicken coop after dark. Some authorities have suggested that if the Negro appears lazy and shiftless to many whites, this may be because he is simply practicing a subtle form of revenge against his oppressor. When he could no longer endure the white, the Negro also found it possible, with the aid of white sympathizers, to flee. During the 40 years before the Civil War, some 75,000 Negroes escaped the South via the Underground Railroad, a clandestine organization of free Negroes and white sympathizers which operated to smuggle slaves to the Northern states and Canada. Many thousands more left their homes during the waves of lynching that followed the war.

As early as 1830 the first National Negro Convention met in Philadelphia to assert the proposition that "all men are born free and equal," and by 1890 there had been similar gatherings in Ohio, California and Texas and in New Orleans and Chicago. The modern history of Negro protest, however, dates from 1905, when a fiery Negro named W. E. B. DuBois organized a group of fellow intellectuals into the Niagara Movement, which was the forerunner of the National Association for the Advancement of Colored People. Highly educated (at Fisk, Harvard and the University of Berlin), with a Vandyke beard and a lofty manner, DuBois rose to prominence as an opponent of Booker T. Washington, the famed Negro educator. Washington, who had founded Tuskegee Institute in 1881, was easily the most prominent Negro in America in the early 1900s. But his counsel to the Negroes that they must first educate themselves and acquire vocational skills before aspiring to the full fruits of freedom—however well intentioned and however much it was welcomed by the whites—did not satisfy militants like DuBois. To them, Booker T. Washington seemed to stamp himself a segregationist when he delivered his famous "separate fingers" speech at the Cotton Exposition in Atlanta in 1895: "In all things that are purely social we can be as separate as the fingers, yet one as the hand in all things essential to mutual progress."

DuBois convened his small young protest group near Niagara Falls (from which the Niagara Movement took its name) in 1905 to encourage Negroes throughout the country to insist on their civil rights. Later a group of white liberals, upset by a bloody race riot in Springfield, Illinois—Abraham Lincoln's own city—proposed to join forces with the Negro group. Thus the NAACP was born, on February 12, 1909, the 100th anniversary of Lincoln's birth. Among the early founders were John Dewey, "the father of modern progressive education," pioneer social worker Jane Addams and journalist Lincoln Steffens. DuBois, who became director of research and publicity, was the only Negro officeholder of the fledgling organization. DuBois broke with the NAACP in 1948. Thirteen years later he joined the Communist Party; then he became a citizen of Ghana and died in Accra at the age of 95, on the day before the Washington march of August 1963.

Throughout much of its early history the NAACP was concerned with trying to end lynching, a form of public terror that accompanied the birth of Jim Crow and which, probably more than any other form of oppression to be found in the South, operated to keep the Negro "in his place." There were times during the black days of the 1890s, it has been reported, when a Negro was lynched every two days in the South, and by the time lynching tapered off in the 1950s, 4,733 cases had been reported.* Contrary to popular impression, not all lynchings were of Negroes who had supposedly raped white women. Women and children were also lynched, and white mobs would resort to lynching for such offenses as a Negro changing jobs, failing to show respect for a white man or attempting to vote. Nor did all their victims die at the end of a rope. In 1916 the white world was shocked by a lynching at Waco, Texas, in which a young Negro mental defective was stabbed and mutilated and then burned alive in the public square while 10,000 people looked on and cheered. An NAACP report at the time noted that the remains of the victim were afterward dragged through the streets and parts sold for souvenirs, his teeth bringing five dollars apiece. Throughout all this, it was the despair of Negro leaders that they were never able to win from Congress a Federal antilynching law, and it was probably moral revulsion as much as anything that finally led to the decline of the practice. But in its place whites have substituted other forms of terror such as shooting into homes and bombings, mostly in the South. Birmingham, Alabama, alone has seen scores of bombings, and one Negro residential section has been the scene of explosions so many times that it is known as Dynamite Hill.

In the meantime, the NAACP had turned its attention to segregation in the public schools with a series of lower-court legal skirmishes. The first of these, filed in 1933 on behalf of a Negro seeking admission to the University of North Carolina, was lost on a technicality, but in 1935 the NAACP succeeded in winning entrance for a Negro into the University of Maryland. There were other victories, and by 1950 the U. S. Supreme

* The last recorded lynching was that of Mack Charles Parker at Poplarville, Mississippi, in 1959. He was accused of kidnaping and raping a white woman.

Court itself, in two decisions, began to strike at the legal structure of segregated education. One of these set the precedent for opening state-operated graduate schools to Negroes. In that same year, however, it seemed to Negro leaders that the court decisions they were winning were too narrowly based and that the gains made for college students were of little help to the great mass of Negro children in the lower schools. At a conference in New York in 1950, NAACP attorneys decided to mount a bold frontal assault on *Plessy* vs. *Ferguson*—the "separate but equal" doctrine—and argue before the Supreme Court that segregation was simply a violation of the U. S. Constitution. A brilliant Baltimore attorney named Thurgood Marshall led the assault, and in 1954 the Supreme Court under Chief Justice Earl Warren struck down the "separate but equal" doctrine and called for integration of the public schools. At long last the Negro seemed on the road to deliverance.

The Negroes had been making gains toward civil rights in other areas too, and a great deal had been happening to the Negro himself. Besides the court decisions affecting education, there had been additional help from the bench. As early as 1915 the Supreme Court had outlawed the grandfather clause, and over the years it also banned segregation in interstate bus travel, buried the white primary and struck at restrictive housing covenants.

Another kind of milestone was recorded in June 1941 when A. Philip Randolph, the founder and president of the Brotherhood of Sleeping Car Porters, threatened a march of 100,000 Negroes on Washington to protest racial discrimination in defense industry employment. Shortly before the march was scheduled to take place, President Franklin D. Roosevelt signed Executive Order 8802, which banned such discrimination. A few weeks later Roosevelt appointed a Fair Employment Practices Commission, and by all accounts the lot of the Negro improved during the years of World War II. Randolph's march never came off, but 22 years later he—with Bayard Rustin—was to lead another great march to Washington.

As it turned out, Congress killed the FEPC in 1946, but by this time the states had begun to act. New York and New

Jersey passed enforceable FEPC laws in 1945, and by 1960 there were similar laws in 21 other states and in 45 cities across the country. As of April 1963, sixteen states and a total of 55 cities also had passed laws dealing, in one way or another, with discrimination in housing. It is another question, however, how beneficial these laws have been. Most deal with public housing, where, for the most part, the resistance of whites is not great. Only ten states and two cities—New York and Pittsburgh—have attempted to come to grips with discrimination in private housing, where white resistance is very much stronger.

The Negro himself, who has been called "the invisible man," * was becoming more visible through widespread acceptance in the fields of entertainment and sports. The first Negro revue, *Dixie to Broadway,* had its debut in New York in 1924, and Duke Ellington opened at the Cotton Club in 1927. Joe Louis, the most widely respected Negro athlete of his time, became heavyweight champion of the world in 1937 and reigned until 1949. Jesse Owens, the great Negro track star, won four gold medals at the Berlin Olympic games of 1936, and Jackie Robinson became the first Negro player in major-league baseball when he joined the Brooklyn Dodgers in 1947. The following year there was another major breakthrough for the Negro when President Harry S. Truman signed Executive Order 9981 ending segregation in the armed forces (A. Philip Randolph had a hand in this too, by threatening a mass civil-disobedience campaign against the draft).

Thus the Negro was inching up the ladder of civil rights, and some of the weapons he would use to telling effect later in his great revolt already were being fashioned. Perhaps of equal importance was the shifting pattern of the Negro's life. Since the turn of the century there had been massive and continuing migrations of Negroes from the South to the North (and increasingly, of late, to the beckoning West). And the Negro population had shifted from predominantly rural to pre-

* From Ralph Ellison's novel, *The Invisible Man,* Random House, New York, 1952.

dominantly urban. The following table illustrates this graphically:

RURAL VS. URBAN NEGRO POPULATION *

Year	Urban (millions)	Rural (millions)
1910	2.7	7.1
1920	3.5	6.9
1930	5.2	6.7
1940	6.2	6.6
1950	9.4	5.6
1960	13.8	5.1

* Source: *Statistical Abstract of the United States,* 1930, 1946, 1962.

This dramatic reversal has not been an unmixed blessing for the Negro. On the one hand he was able—particularly in the urban North—to savor the rewards of relatively less discrimination and to enjoy a measure of political power. But all too often he was forced to live in a ghetto, and increasingly he was outrunning the availability of unskilled jobs. With burgeoning automation he was also encountering the old bugaboo of "last hired, first fired." * The urbanization of the Negro, however, served both to sharpen his own mood of rebellion and to dramatize his plight before the white world.

This was the Negro's situation when the Supreme Court gave its important decision of 1954. It seemed that the Negro was finally on his way, but, as after the Civil War, he was doomed to wait again. The South received the court's ruling with outraged cries ("National suicide," thundered Georgia's Governor Herman Talmadge) and rushed to erect a barrier of local laws to preserve segregation. In 1955 the alarmed Supreme Court

* In the fall of 1963, Leon Greenburg of the U.S. Department of Labor released a study showing that some 200,000 jobs were being lost each year to automation. Though there was no breakdown of how many of these affected Negroes, the Department of Labor has reported that blue-collar jobs for Negroes have "diminished steadily during the postwar period as a result of automation and other technological developments."

buttressed its decision with an order that desegregation of the schools should proceed "with all deliberate speed." The NAACP then began the laborious task of going to the lower courts so as to force action from white officials. At Mansfield, Texas, in 1956, white mobs prevented Negroes from entering a high school; the National Guard was needed to quell violence at Clinton, Tennessee, and Sturgis, Kentucky. Autherine Lucy entered the Deep South University of Alabama in 1956 to the accompaniment of riots. She was later expelled, and the University of Alabama did not again become a target of the Negroes until 1963. The following year, the new Hattie Cotton elementary school at Nashville, Tennessee, was bombed to rubble.

The year 1957 also brought Little Rock. The siege of Little Rock's Central High School was, in many ways, a classic study of the Negro's effort to end segregation in the Southern schools. First there were the long, careful maneuvers in the courts by the NAACP to prepare the way for nine students to enter Central High in the 1957–58 school year; then the defiance by local authority in the person of Governor Orval Faubus; the violence of the white populace; and, ultimately, the intervention of Federal troops dispatched by President Dwight D. Eisenhower to escort the Negro children to their classes. It was a pattern that, with variations, was to be repeated in many places throughout the South and to be climaxed in 1962 with the terrible riot, bloodshed and death that accompanied the entry of James Meredith into the University of Mississippi at Oxford, Mississippi.

In the battle-scarred history of the Negro revolution since the 1954 Supreme Court decision, Oxford was a nightmare. For two horrible days—Sunday, September 30, and Monday, October 1—the battle raged, with upward of 2,500 frenzied whites repeatedly charging the Federal marshals, the federalized Mississippi National Guard and the Regular Army troops who protected the seething campus. A hundred years before, in the fall of 1862, Ole Miss had felt the tramp of Federal boots when Ulysses S. Grant, on his drive deep into the state, billeted his troops on the campus. If this was ground hallowed in U.S. history, it trembled now to exploding tear-gas bombs and the screams of the whites: "Give us the nigger!" In the holocaust two men, a French journalist and a local Oxford resident, fell dead and at least 375 were injured. But in the end, defiant Governor Ross Barnett yielded and James Meredith entered the university. In 1963 Meredith was graduated.

The great disappointment for the Negro was that all of his tortured effort and apparent success were really availing him very little. Not always was there violence and not always were Federal troops and marshals needed, but it became all too evident that the grudging South—even when pressed to the limit—was yielding no more than token integration of its schools. At the extreme, as in Prince Edward County, Virginia, some Southerners were willing to see their schools closed rather than be tainted with Negroes. Integration there was, but at such a snail's pace that it was measured in fractions of percentage points a year. At the beginning of the 1963–64 school year an estimated .8 per cent of Southern Negro pupils were attending integrated classes. And it is interesting to note that, as of June 1963, all the early pain of Little Rock had resulted in only 69 Negroes—out of some 7,700 students—attending the supposedly integrated junior and senior high schools of that city.

Toward the end of the 1950s the slow progress of school integration had begun to anger many Negroes, and there were cries against the caution of the NAACP with its patient plodding through the courts. As Louis Lomax was to write: "The NAACP's troubling is born of the fact that . . . events . . . have shaken our faith in legalism as a tool of deliverance; we now want our major civil rights organization to look beyond the courts to the people themselves as the final and quick arbiters of public policy."

What now came to the fore was the new—though, in reality, old—weapon of direct mass action. The effectiveness of concerted action by the Negroes had been demonstrated earlier when a young Baptist minister named Martin Luther King, Jr., waged the successful boycott of local bus lines in Montgomery, Alabama, in 1955–56. King, with his Gandhi-inspired philosophy of direct, nonviolent mass protest, was to form the

militant Southern Christian Leadership Conference shortly afterward and go on to become the pre-eminent leader of the Negro
revolution. At the time, however, mass action did not catch
hold, and it wasn't until 1960, when a group of students sat
down at a lunch counter in Greensboro, North Carolina, that the
Negro demonstrations as we know them today began in earnest.

The date was February 1, 1960. The night before, a Sunday,
McNeil A. Joseph, a 17-year-old student at the all-Negro
Agricultural and Technical College of North Carolina in
Greensboro, had been brooding about discrimination and wondering what he could do about it ("Segregation makes me feel
that I'm unwanted," Joseph explained later). The next morning he approached three of his fellow students and proposed
that they go downtown after classes and demand service at
the lunch counter of the Woolworth store. Their sit-in began
at 4:45 in the afternoon when, after making small purchases
at other counters, they sat down at the white lunch counter
and asked for service. When they were refused they took out
their textbooks and studied until the store closed at 5:30.

Nothing much really happened at Greensboro that day.
But the sit-in of McNeil Joseph—which was entirely his own
spontaneous idea—caught on like wildfire all over the South
with Negro students who were fed up with the slow progress
of their leaders. In less than two weeks the student sit-ins had
spread to fifteen other cities; at the end of the month they had
reached 33, and on and on. Asked why the sit-ins had spread
so rapidly, the NAACP's Thurgood Marshall replied good-
humoredly: "If you mean are the young people impatient with
me, the answer is yes."

The great attraction and success of the early sit-ins, however,
were by no means lost on the Negro leadership. The Rev.
Martin Luther King, Jr., rushed forward to lend a hand to the
students, as did the NAACP and another existing organization
of which the nation would hear much, the Congress of Racial
Equality.

CORE had been formed in Chicago in 1942 by a group
headed by James L. Farmer, a former program director of the
NAACP who became CORE's national director. Farmer had

been reading *War Without Violence* by Krishnalal Shridharanai
—a disciple of Gandhi—and was intrigued with the idea of
applying its concept of passive resistance to the Negro revolt.
The first use of it was at the now defunct Jack Spratt restaurant
in Chicago in 1942. CORE was a militant new note in the
struggle: "Our function," Marvin Rich, CORE's community
relations director, has said, "is to translate law and morality
into practice. We need people willing to take risks." But it was
not the only one. As a direct result of the 1960 sit-ins, the
Student Nonviolent Coordinating Committee (SNCC, pronounced Snick) was formed in that year to bring some kind
of organization to the student protests. Headed by two young
Negroes—executive secretary James Forman, a young Chicagoan, and chairman John Lewis—SNCC has been perhaps
the most militant of all Negro organizations and has seen thousands of its staff and associates go to jail—often for their efforts
to encourage Negro voter registration.

The proliferation of Negro leadership organizations points
up a significant fact of the Negro's revolution: that it has lacked
any clear-cut, centralized direction. Although Martin Luther
King, Jr., has come closest to being the Negro's symbolic
leader, no one individual or organization has been able to
presume to speak for all Negroes, nor, always, to control their
triumphant surge into the streets. The same proliferation has,
despite official disclaimers, undoubtedly led to some rivalry
among the groups—for headlines and money, and over how
best to wage the fight. When it was under fire for its legalistic
approach, the NAACP retorted that it was all very well for
the young Negroes to go around getting themselves jailed, but
it was the NAACP that had to bail them out and fight their
court cases. Roy Wilkins, the NAACP's national director, has
said: "[They] furnish the noise" in racial protests while the
NAACP "pays the bills." Wilkins said of CORE, SNCC and
SCLC, "here today and gone tomorrow. There is only one
organization that can handle a long, sustained fight—the
NAACP."

Yet the vibrant, headlong rush of the militant groups was
immensely appealing to Negroes everywhere. Pressed on by

youthful members of its own organization, the NAACP, by the time of its national convention in Chicago in 1963, was itself calling for more demonstrations.

Indeed, it seemed that these could hardly be stopped. The sit-ins of 1960 were followed by the often bloody Freedom Rides of 1961, when the Negroes (and white supporters) rode directly into brutal violence. As variations on a theme, there were wade-ins at beaches and swim-ins at pools, kneel-ins at churches and lie-ins at construction projects. By early 1963 the pace of the Negro revolution was quickening rapidly. And then there occurred an event that made all earlier developments seem merely a prologue: the riots of Birmingham, Alabama.

In the spring, when Martin Luther King, Jr., proposed to protest discrimination in Birmingham with the most massive marches yet seen in the South, there were those Negroes who were skeptical. The city was on the threshold of installing a new government which gave promise of being more moderate, and it seemed prudent to wait. Yet King, believing firmly that "now is the time," did not wait. By the thousands the Negroes marched and by the thousands they were arrested. Although he was severely criticized in white quarters, King even threw Negro children into the fray. And, though no one could say they were not goaded into it, for one of the few times in all their struggles the Negroes struck back. This was on a sultry Saturday night in May when the home of the Rev. A. D. King, brother of Martin Luther King, and the command post of King himself were bombed. For the next five hours, in retaliation, the Negroes boiled through the streets, wielding knives, overturning cars, hurling rocks and bricks at anyone who moved, even other Negroes. One wounded Negro moaned: "They were insane."

Yet the fame and the significance of Birmingham do not rest on its being the biggest demonstration up to that time or the fact that the Negroes themselves became violent, but on an image: Public Safety Commissioner Eugene (Bull) Connor, who seemed to symbolize all that was intransigent about the white South, chose to turn loose his dogs and his fire hoses on the marchers. It has been said that when the dogs bit into the black man in Birmingham, "every Negro in the world bled." So also did the dogs prick the conscience of many a white in America. For the Negro, after Birmingham, there was no turning back. And for the white man there seemed no escape.

But there was more to come. In June, while Governor George Wallace of Alabama breathed defiance, two young Negroes, Vivian Malone and James Hood, were scheduled to enter the University of Alabama at Tuscaloosa, where Autherine Lucy had been expelled seven years earlier. Alabama also stood as the only state left in the Union without a single integrated school, and the situation seemed ominous enough that President John F. Kennedy put his brother, Robert F. Kennedy, in charge of Federal intervention. Attorney General Kennedy's resources included a force of Federal marshals and 400 riot-trained Army troops poised in helicopters at Fort Benning, Georgia. They were not needed. For although Governor Wallace made a pretense of barring the door, Vivian Malone and James Hood entered the university without incident.*

Tuscaloosa, however, served to point up the growing involvement of the U.S. Government in the civil-rights struggle. In 1956 President Eisenhower had declined to intervene in the Autherine Lucy affair, but a year later, at Little Rock, he was obliged to use Federal troops. President Kennedy also had used troops in real emergencies, but though he had campaigned in 1960 with promises of civil-rights legislation, he had done very little to deliver it. Now the President called for new civil-rights legislation, including a public-accommodations law, and he did something else that no other U.S. President had ever done: He appealed directly to all the nation to end discrimination against the Negro. In a nationally televised address, Kennedy told the United States that it faced nothing less than a moral crisis, both as a country and as a people. "It cannot," said the President, "be met by repressive police action. It cannot be left to increased demonstrations in the streets. It cannot be quieted by token moves or talk. It is time to act in

* A few months later, Hood resigned, citing reasons of health.

the Congress, in your state and local legislative body, and, above all, in all of our daily lives."

Almost nothing that had happened to the Negroes in the last ten years, the *Newsweek* poll clearly established, heartened them quite so much as the President's speech. Over and over they expressed wonderment that the President of the United States had actually gone on television in their behalf. Finally and irrevocably the leader of their country had told the nation that their cause was right and just and should be fulfilled.

Seven hours after the President finished speaking, Medgar Evers, an NAACP field worker, was shot and killed from ambush in Jackson, Mississippi.

And now the tempo of the Negro protest rose even higher in what Negro leaders came to call "the summer of our discontent." Demonstrations erupted all over the country, North and South, and not even the city halls of New York or Chicago were immune. In a three-month period of the summer of 1963, the U.S. Justice Department counted 1,412 separate demonstrations. The newspaper pictures showing the limp bodies of Negroes being carried to police patrol wagons became a great tapestry of the times. Over the land echoed the Negro hymn "We Shall Overcome." Now the revolution was indeed in full stride, and it rushed pell-mell to the grand climax of that summer: the march on Washington of August 28, 1963.

There were, beforehand, those skeptics who said that the grand march would achieve the Negro nothing, and there were those who feared that it would erupt into naked and terrible violence. These criticisms were soon lost in what actually happened. By train and bus and plane and even roller skates, and from all parts of the country, the Negroes and their white supporters came—reportedly some 210,000 strong and with proud old A. Philip Randolph and Bayard Rustin at their head. Massed before the Lincoln Memorial, the throngs were orderly and the voices of their speakers temperate. There would, no doubt, be much more grief and travail before the Negro ever won his full rights, but, for the time, Washington bespoke the growing dignity and the growing maturity of his revolution.

At the end of a long day, Martin Luther King, Jr., rose and

delivered his famous "I have a dream" speech to the multitudes. Twenty years before, Gunnar Myrdal had observed that the Negro problem was not only America's greatest failure but incomparably its greatest opportunity. And he, too, spoke of a dream.

"If America," wrote Myrdal, "should follow its own deepest convictions, its well-being at home would be increased directly. At the same time America's prestige and power abroad would rise immensely. The century-old dream of American patriots, that America should give to the entire world its own freedoms and its own faith, would come true."

CHAPTER 3

WHAT IT'S LIKE TO BE A NEGRO

If you think it don't hurt, you are wrong. —An unemployed man in Detroit, Michigan.

ONE OF THE Negro's enduring complaints, voiced over and over again in the *Newsweek* poll, is "if they would only get to know us they would see we are not so bad." This is at once a hard statement of the facts of life for a Negro as well as an expression of hope for the future.

Negroes believe whites don't understand them, don't understand what it is like to be discriminated against and segregated. If they did, they could not have kept the Negro bound in the chains of discrimination for a hundred years. Its effects on the spirit are deep and shameful, the Negro feels. Why, he wants to know, must he be a second-class citizen in a land that prides itself on fair treatment for all? Why can't he have the same chance for homes and jobs and education as the white man? What in Heaven's name is the matter with him, he asks, that makes him so inferior to the white race? James Baldwin has observed: "You were born where you were born and faced the future that you faced because you were black and *for no other reason* [italics his]. You were born into a society which spelled out with brutal clarity, and in as many ways as possible, that you were a worthless human being." *

Although the Negro's everyday concern is with discrimination in such specific areas as jobs and schools, he feels very keenly the basic, general humiliation of being considered worthless by the whites around him. It is this that Negroes feel the white man doesn't understand. A segregated world, many Negroes point out, is often a lonely and a frightening world. How can the whites possibly know, they ask, what it means to be traveling, with night falling and the children tired, and have to drive a hundred or more miles more than you intend in order to find a place that will give Negroes accommodations? How, they ask, can the whites know what it means to arrive in a strange city and stand on the street corner wondering where you can go to eat, or sleep, and not be turned away? How do you know where to get such an everyday thing as a haircut?

Whatever one might think of the Black Muslims, their New York leader, Malcolm X, had a point when he told *Newsweek* that no white could possibly understand the empathy which passes between two Negroes when they exchange glances or simply say, "Man."

It was precisely to sound the depths of the Negro's feeling about his second-class status that the poll directed this question to him: "During your whole lifetime, as far as you personally are concerned, if you had to name one thing, how has discrimination affected you the most?"

The effect of this question was like touching a raw nerve end for the vast majority of Negroes surveyed. In almost no other part of the poll was there such a variety or wealth of response. Clearly this was a question that called up ringing echoes from a whole lifetime. What came out were poignant, intimate glimpses of what discrimination has done to the black man.

* *The Fire Next Time*, Dial Press, New York, 1963.

The survey among the rank and file showed that discrimination makes its impact early in life.

A Detroit physician recalled, "I had to walk five miles when I went to school in Virginia. I passed three white schools on the way to this broken-down school." "As a kid I hated myself because I was black, because black to me meant the other side of the tracks, third-class citizenship—the person who had to take the brunt of the jokes," observed Richard Macon, a teacher of Detroit. "In my school days," recalled William Turner of Chicago, "I was scared to death by a bunch of whites who wanted to kill me."

For those Negroes who have borne arms for their country there were often unpleasant recollections of their treatment in uniform, at least before the armed forces were desegregated in 1948. To many of the more than one million Negroes who served in World War II, the services offered better food, clothing and pay than they had ever known. Yet all too often they were relegated to the hard jobs of road building and truck driving, or the boring routine of guarding airplanes. It is probable that their memories of life in the service have dimmed with the passage of time, but some still recall their wartime duty as the supreme irony of discrimination: being asked to die for a country that does not accept you. Speaking for those Negroes, Charlie Jones of Chicago put it this way: "I had whites to spit at me and scream 'nigger.' I was headed overseas for duty and the thought of fighting and possibly dying for nothing made me feel that I was fighting without a cause." Quite a few other Negroes mentioned that their great disillusionment came when they returned from the service to find that nothing had been changed by their donning a uniform—they were still unwanted.

Discrimination has placed a special burden on Negro parents. Theirs is the immensely difficult task of explaining discrimination to children born without prejudice or knowledge that their black skins make a difference. At the same time the parents must, if they can, try to forestall in their young the feeling of inferiority that very often is the consequence of discrimination. How, to repeat Dr. Byron Biscoe's poignant question, do you explain to the black child that he can't take the white's pony ride or sit up front and watch the fascinating maneuvers of the bus driver? And how, many Negroes ask, do you soothe the child's disappointment or convince him that he is not inferior when these experiences are repeated over and over? The Negroes themselves do not profess to have any hard answers to these questions, save to lay the facts of discrimination squarely before their children. They are aware, too, that their economic plight makes it difficult even to raise children. This is so not only because of inadequate diet or crowded living quarters but very often because of the absence of a mother who is at work. As of March 1960, close to half (41 per cent) of all nonwhite married women were working, compared with less than a third (30 per cent) of white married women. In fact, according to the U.S. Census Bureau, more than one-third (34 per cent) of all nonwhite mothers with children under six years of age find it necessary to work, while only 19 per cent of white mothers with small children are counted in the nation's labor force. As a New York City teacher's aide put it: "White people . . . have forced us to scrub their floors and look after their children and leave ours uncared for."

The rank-and-file Negroes in the survey poured out a flood of variations on the theme of discrimination. Many recalled a specific incident or encounter from daily life as the thing that had bothered them most:

"It makes me mad when I have to wait to be waited on in a department store while the clerk waits on a white woman, even if I got there first"—a 28-year-old woman in Washington, D.C.

"I have gone in places only to be told they don't serve Negroes or they don't hire Negroes, and if you think that don't hurt, you are wrong"—an unemployed man in Detroit.

"I have been denied certain privileges in traveling and eating places, when I have had the money to pay for what I wanted"—a retired Army chaplain of West Palm Beach, Florida.

"They send you to the back, call you 'nigger' and stuff like that"—an Augusta, Ga., housewife.

"The signs around that say 'White Only'—that bugs me most of all"—Earbie Bledsoe of St. Louis, Missouri.

"I . . . can't go out for nice entertainment, can't use bathrooms in stores after buying"—a 31-year-old housewife of Baton Rouge, Louisiana.

"Living in the South all my life, I can't single out one thing. Everything about it makes me mad"—a Washington, D.C., housewife.

A good many other Negroes had trouble singling out a specific example of how discrimination has hurt them the most. They groped to explain their feeling: wounded pride, perhaps, or an outraged sense of justice. More than a few were able to recognize that their status as second-class citizens had done something to them—warped their personalities, or embittered them. A dentist in Oklahoma commented on these less visible effects: "Some people place the emphasis on the wallet, but you can decimate a people by depriving them of the opportunity to see a play and hear good music. An individual should not be so stifled."

Here are other observations of rank-and-file Negroes to whom the psychological consequences of discrimination are the most important:

"Since I have been indoctrinated as a Negro that I am inferior, I have begun to ask myself if and why I am inferior. This is the most damaging personality conflict for the Negro" —Mrs. Evelyn Bryant of Detroit, Michigan.

"I know it has affected me somehow, but I can't put my finger on it. I think that it has given me a subconscious hostility to whites"—a journalist in New Orleans, Louisiana.

"It has made me bitter and pessimistic"—Stephanie S. Cabaniss of Washington, D.C.

"It has caused me to have inhibitions about myself. It has caused me to walk lightly or pretend I don't know, in order to get along"—Mrs. Ruth Turpin of Detroit, Michigan.

There was very little difference between the reaction of the rank and file and the 100 Negroes who were chosen for the leadership sample of the survey. Jim Crow in all its ugly forms touches them too, and in much the same ways as it does the rank and file. They too have felt discrimination in their everyday lives, or in its psychological effects. "When I was going to school," State Senator Basil W. Brown of Michigan recalled, "I used to work summers [as] a janitor. That's all I could get— any Negro could get—while the rest of my white buddies were running machines."

There was, however, one major difference between the way the leadership group looked at discrimination and the way the rank and file did. For some leaders, discrimination itself has been the stimulus, the goad, that drove them to their positions of eminence in the Negro society. Thus, James L. Farmer, the national director of CORE, commented: "Discrimination increased my determination to do something about inferiority feelings. I felt handicapped, but never doubted my own ability." Ernest Calloway, Associate Research Director of the Central Conference of Teamsters in St. Louis, put it this way: "Discrimination has challenged me—to prove how wrong it is." A few leaders even saw real spiritual value to the experience of discrimination. For example, the Rev. S. Leon Whitney, a Baptist minister of Jackson, Mississippi, observed: "Discrimination has given me an appreciation and an understanding of the underdog, of people all over the world who are struggling for first-class citizenship. This may sound ironic, but segregation has taught me the meaning of freedom."

These, then, are the feelings of the Negroes—in their own words—about discrimination. They comprise a kaleidoscope of human emotion, from the snub of going unwaited on in a department store to the fear of death. How well the Negro is able to describe his encounters with discrimination depends on the amount of his education and, to some extent at least, on the degree of his sensitivity as a person. But no matter how it is described, discrimination is felt by the large majority of Negroes. Only 13 per cent of rank-and-file Negroes, and only a tiny 4 per cent of the leadership group, said it had not affected them at all. Fourteen per cent of rank-and-file Negroes (and 1 per cent of the leaders) claimed not to know how discrimination has affected them. Predictably, the "don't know" figure was highest for low-income slum dwellers of the North (25 per cent) and the rural Negroes of the South (22 per cent). Overall, therefore, three out of four rank-and-file Negroes and very nearly all of the leaders know quite well what discrimination is and how it has twisted their lives.

Aside from the general, personal feelings of inferiority and frustration which discrimination may give the Negro, it affects him in three main areas: jobs, education and housing. The most important of these, according to the survey, is employment.

EMPLOYMENT

Answering the poll's question of how discrimination has affected them most in their lifetime, 30 per cent of rank-and-file Negroes and 26 per cent of the leaders listed employment. And, for those who like to believe that the North is more tolerant than the South, it is interesting to note that the percentage of all Negroes unhappy about jobs and wages was higher for the North than for the South.

In the case of jobs, of course, the Negroes begin with a disadvantage, because in mid-1963, 13.3 per cent of them were unemployed. This was twice as high as the national average of 6.1 per cent. Moreover, the wages they are paid have almost always been depressed. In July of 1963 the U.S. Census Bureau reported to the Senate subcommittee on Employment and Manpower that though the Negro's wage has risen in absolute terms, it has not kept pace at all with white wages for the last twenty years. The high in recent years for the Negro was 1951, when his median wage was $2,060 a year, or 62 per cent of the white median of $3,345. By 1962 the Negro's wage was up to $3,023, but this was only 55 per cent of white earnings of $5,462. Thus, the Negro's wage is showing an alarming tendency to decline, relative to whites, and in a very real sense he has hardly shared in the general prosperity of the nation.

The Negroes know all this better than anyone else. But more than that, they are convinced that even when they have a job and do equal work with a white, they won't—because of discrimination—be paid as much as the white man. In the poll they were asked if, doing the same work as a white man, they thought they would be paid the same or less. More than half of the rank and file answered "less." Disenchantment with wages was highest in the South and highest of all among rural Southern Negroes at 66 per cent. Predictably, there was less pessimism among the Negro leaders, many of whom already have adequate jobs; still, almost half of the leaders thought they would be paid less. Here is a summarized table of their views:

NEGROES ASSESS CHANCES OF EQUAL PAY FOR EQUAL WORK

	Total Rank and File	Non-South	South	Leaders
	%	%	%	%
Same pay as whites	33	43	25	43
Less pay	56	47	63	48
Not sure	11	10	12	9

Not only does the Negro suffer when it comes to wages, but he is highly discriminated against in the kinds of jobs he can hold, as well as in other areas of employment practices. In its 1961 report, the U.S. Commission on Civil Rights found discrimination against Negroes in vocational training, in apprenticeship training programs, by labor organizations—particularly the construction and machinists' crafts—and by the referral services of state employment offices.

In the *Newsweek* sample, fully 34 per cent of rank-and-file Negroes reported that they were employed as unskilled laborers or in domestic or other service occupations. Only 4 per cent were skilled laborers and only 2 per cent could class themselves as businessmen. However, largely owing to the many all-Negro schools in both the North and South, a respectable 9 per cent were teachers.

Because of their downtrodden job status, the Negroes are able to pinpoint very well the occupations where they are wanted and where they are not wanted. Asked which trades or fields give them the worst break, the rank and file named skilled labor first (by 13 per cent), then white-collar jobs (12 per cent) and the construction trades (10 per cent) as the most discriminatory. On the reverse side of the coin, they named government and civil-service jobs as the fields where they get the best break (19 per cent), followed by social work and teaching positions (13 per cent).

Reflecting either his exclusion from organized labor or his lack of qualifications for membership, only one in five Negroes said that he belonged to a union.

The Negro is highly vocal about prejudice on the job. "You know," said a 52-year-old unemployed Chicagoan, "just the other day, fellow told me they fired one Negro and hired five white men. When the unemployment man sees me come into the office, he don't even come over. He just goes and sits down." "Most of them don't want you if they can get a white person," said a middle-aged woman on welfare in Washington, D.C. "Just read the want ads. Whites only." A St. Louis, Missouri, housewife put it this way: "For every kind of job there is, the whites get a better break."

EDUCATION

Education was the second most prevalent area of discrimination, listed by 11 per cent of the rank and file. Education scored highest (23 per cent) among middle- and upper-income Negroes of the North, who have seen at first hand the value of an education in competing for jobs. However, education rated only 13 per cent among the Negro leaders, who in the main already have the benefit of higher education.

Probably in no other area do all the forces of discrimination combine so damagingly as in the education of the Negro. Segregated schooling has been the Negro's heritage in the South and *de facto* segregation is a familiar contrivance of some Northern cities. This is their starting point; when compounded by all the other depressing circumstances of discrimination, many Negro children are left with no incentive to continue their education.

It is true that in the primary grades the Negroes have made rapid progress. In 1940, 91.2 per cent of Negro children ages 7 to 13 were attending school. By 1960, according to the U.S. Department of Labor, virtually all of them were. But the Negroes also have shown an ominous tendency to drop out of high school, where they have the best chance to prepare themselves for a job or to go on to colleges and professional schools.

High-school dropout figures are hard to come by, but some

studies suggest that the rate for Negroes may be very nearly twice as high as for whites. In the survey, 10 per cent—or close to one in ten—of all Negroes reported that one or more children in their family had dropped out of high school. The reasons they gave were an accumulation of the Negro's woes: breakdown of morals or parental control caused by broken homes and working mothers; poor homes and living conditions; poverty that compels the child to go to work in order to help feed himself; and, above all, lack of incentive, because the child is sure that no worthwhile job awaits him when he graduates. Thus, a Mt. Vernon, New York, housewife told of her own experience: "They feel they don't have a chance, so why struggle? I got honors in high school but I can't get a decent job."

Quite a few Negroes saw the lack of incentive as a self-perpetuating problem: If the parents haven't had an education, they see no need for it. "In many homes there is no love of learning—thus there can be no help from them," said George S. Schuyler, New York journalist. Another type of problem was mentioned by a 29-year-old waiter in Jackson, Mississippi: "The young girls are getting pregnant—trying to get grown too quick."

By an overwhelming majority, 98 per cent, the Negroes want their children to stay in school, for they are convinced that education is the ladder of upward progress. But they are not nearly so sure that, even when he stays in school, the Negro gets as good an education as the white in present circumstances. Very nearly half (48 per cent) of rank-and-file Negroes think that the education of their children is inferior to whites. Predictably, condemnation of the schools is highest in the segregated South, as the following table shows:

NEGROES ASSESS QUALITY OF EDUCATION RECEIVED BY CHILDREN

	Total Rank and File %	Non-South %	South %	Leaders %
As good as whites	35	47	25	52
Inferior to whites	48	33	60	40
Not sure	17	20	15	8

Negroes are convinced that the whites have better facilities, better teachers, better curricula, even better books. Not all feel this way—some blame Negro parents themselves for a lack of interest in the education of their children—but the majority do. These were typical comments from both the rank and file and the leadership group:

"Several little white girls I know can say ABCs and other things and they're in kindergarten just like mine, but she doesn't know as much"—a young woman who cleans offices in Houston, Texas.

"Some of the Negro teachers are not trained properly. The young girls today go into teaching because they are in demand and are guaranteed a job"—a 30-year-old landscape gardener of Chicago.

"I was raised in the country and we got the books white children had used in the fifth grade when we were in the seventh grade"—a 22-year-old construction worker of Houston, Texas.

"The curriculum is not the same. The financial output is not the same. Anything that is separate is inherently unequal"—the Rev. A. K. Stanley, Greensboro, North Carolina.

"When white children come home they have five to six books. Well, my children don't have any books to bring home. Not only my children but all the Negroes"—a 36-year-old housemaid of Miami.

HOUSING

The survey found that the Negro is unhappy about discrimination in housing but does not rate it on a par with discrimination in jobs or education. Replying to the question of how discrimination has affected them most, only 3 per cent of the rank and file and 1 per cent of the leaders named housing. The figure was highest (6 per cent) among low-income Negroes of the North, whose lot in the big cities, more often than not, is the ghetto.

Why was this? Nothing could be more obvious to the Negro than the fact that he is all too often discriminated against in housing. The black slums of Harlem and the South Side of

Chicago—to name but two—are the plainest evidence of that. Recent figures provided by the National Urban League show that one out of every six Negro dwelling units is dilapidated, obsolete or otherwise substandard, as compared with one in 32 white dwelling units. Sixty-six per cent of white families in America own their own homes, but only 38 per cent of Negro families do. Because of lower incomes, Negroes make heavy use of public housing; as of 1963, 49 per cent of all Federal public housing was occupied by Negroes.

The poll graphically showed the substandard housing plight of the Negro. Among low-income Negroes outside the South, for example, only 31 per cent have a bathtub; among rural Negroes of the South, only 59 per cent. Similarly, only two out of five low-income Negroes of the North have hot water in their dwellings and eight in ten have an inside toilet. Rural Southern Negroes fare better on the availability of hot water, at more than half, but only two out of three have an inside toilet. By contrast all in the leadership group have hot water and bathtub, while 93 per cent have inside toilets.

Since the Negro very often does not have the means to buy a house, and very often, too, is denied mortgage credit because of his status, he must rent. And he is convinced, the poll showed, that when he rents a house or an apartment, he must pay more for it than a white would for the same accommodation:

NEGROES ASSESS RENTS THEY WOULD PAY COMPARED TO WHITES

	Rank and File %	Leaders %
Same rent	30	20
More rent	53	76
Not sure	17	4

Over half of the rank-and-file Negroes thus believed that they would pay more rent. This conviction was strongest, as a further breakdown showed, among upper- and middle-income Negroes of the North (84 per cent). That the Negro is right in his surmise can scarcely be questioned. In a ghetto like New York's Harlem, it is common for Negroes to be asked to pay $110 a month for a miserable two or three rooms. The U.S. Civil Rights Commission has reported that, in general, the Negro pays a "color tax" of $5 to $20 per room over what whites pay for the same kind of housing.*

Considering all this, why is it, then, that the Negroes resent discrimination so much more in jobs and schools than they do in housing?

The real answer, of course, is that when it comes to housing —or indeed for any part of his discriminated life—the Negro knows that discrimination feeds upon itself. He recognizes that poverty begets poverty, that he needs a better job before he can buy a better house. When Negroes look at all the forces of discrimination affecting their lives, they single out jobs and the education necessary to get them as the touchstones to a better life.

We have seen, thus far, that Negroes feel discrimination deeply, both as a personal grievance and in its effect on their livelihoods. But how deeply do they feel it?

One of the most startling results of the survey was the finding that a fair number of Negroes are so bitter that they are not sure they would defend their own homeland.

In his feelings about his country, the Negro displays a curious ambivalence. When asked what country in the world gives minorities the fairest break, 21 per cent named the United States. This was a far larger vote of confidence than any other country received. In large measure, of course, this answer represents ignorance of the minority situation in other countries. But

* On the other hand, the *Newsweek* poll established that not many Negroes feel that they are the victims of price gouging in other areas, as in the goods they buy. Seventy per cent of the rank and file and 86 per cent of the leaders felt that they pay the same price as whites for most of the things they buy. Their explanation is that with nationally advertised brands and standardized chain stores, price gouging is not easy. They do feel, however, that they often get an inferior *quality* of merchandise, as in meats and produce, for their money as compared with whites.

in part, too, it is a reflection of the Negro's belief that, even with all its faults, the United States is still the best.

Yet when Negroes were asked if they thought the United States was worth fighting for in a war, about one in five answered either that it was not, or that they were not sure. Moreover, there were no significant geographical distinctions in this feeling, as the following table shows:

NEGRO WILLINGNESS TO FIGHT FOR THE U.S.A.

	Non-South %	South %	All Negroes %
Worth fighting for	82	80	81
Not worth it	10	8	9
Not sure	8	12	10

In his *The Fire Next Time,* James Baldwin rather startled the country when he wrote that "there are some wars . . . that the American Negro will not support." In May of 1963 Baldwin told U.S. Attorney General Robert F. Kennedy much the same thing, to Kennedy's amazed disbelief. It may well be that Baldwin overstated the case, but he obviously had sensed the disenchantment of many of his people. Here are a few comments which support his view:

"I wouldn't fight as things are now. I fought once for freedom and didn't get it. It was 'Go back, Nigger, where you belong' "—Willie Baker of Savannah, Georgia.

"Just leave me out. If you are going to leave me out in the good, leave me out in the bad"—an 80-year-old man of Jackson, Mississippi.

"There's no stripe in the flag for the Negro. If he fights for his country, he should have a stripe"—an unemployed man in Wichita, Kansas.

Even among the majority who would fight, their answers sometimes revealed reservations:

"Sure, I'd fight, I was born here. However, my patriotism is very low"—Givens Bryant of San Diego, California.

"I'd fight as an American, but I lost a brother and I don't know what for"—Luria Jones of New York City.

A number of Negroes linked their willingness to fight with their own struggle and hopes for the future. "I feel that this is my country, worth fighting for just because I have a right to protest the treatment I'm getting," said St. Louis alderman William L. Clay. And ex-baseball star Jackie Robinson believed that "For our stake in the future we've got to fight. Our stake is very great."

To be sure, the Negroes have made progress against discrimination, notably the better-off Negroes of the North who increasingly have won admission to good restaurants, white-collar jobs, and decent neighborhoods. But this has been more from sufferance, or from the profit motive of white proprietors or landlords, than as a matter of *right*. The fact is that no other minority has been forced to walk so deeply in the shadow of U.S. life—relegated to the poorest jobs and the poorest schools and the poorest homes, but, more than that, shunned and looked down on by vast numbers of his fellow men. The cruel anomaly for the Negro is that all this has happened to him in a land dedicated since its very inception to the principle of freedom for all, regardless of race, creed or color. In the survey, many Negroes cried out that they weren't asking for any favors, any radical or fundamental change in the basic tenets of America. All they really wanted were the rights long ago guaranteed to them and so long deferred. By the 1960s it was painfully obvious to the Negro—if to no one else—that law without implementation is not only meaningless but mockery. It was then that he took matters into his own hands in an ever-rising tide of protest, and began slowly but inexorably to fight free of his bonds.

CHAPTER 4

WEAPONS
OF THE
REVOLUTION

IT WAS A WARM Saturday in Montgomery, Alabama, but there was the hint of a cool breeze under the leafy elms on South Court Street. The hour was 10:23 A.M., and at that precise moment the blue-and-silver Greyhound bus, with a sigh of air brakes, pulled into the buff-brick depot from Birmingham.

Stepping down from the bus were nineteen college students, sixteen of them Negro and three of them white, who were part of a new breed of civil-rights demonstrators calling themselves Freedom Riders. For the first few minutes after their arrival they were besieged by reporters firing questions and photographers popping flashbulbs in their faces. And then a band of white men and women burst into the station and advancd on the little group of students and press. A heavy-set white man with a dead cigar in his teeth stepped up to Moe Levy, a photographer for NBC-TV, and slapped him heavily in the face.

As the white attackers advanced, more pressmen were pummeled until suddenly a white woman screamed, "Get those niggers!"

What happened next was a bloody riot—ugly, seething, all restraint on the part of the whites gone. The Freedom Riders gave ground until they were backed against an iron railing at the edge of a ten-foot dropoff to a driveway below. Savagely the whites pushed some of them over the railing and bodily hurled others down. One of the Riders, a 21-year-old white student named James Zwerg, was trapped by several men and slugged until his face was a mass of blood. And then while the men held Zwerg, white women came up to batter him with their fists and their purses. Time after time Zwerg slumped to the ground, only to be kicked in the face and groin. Barely conscious, he staggered to a driverless taxicab and found refuge inside.

But now, with the first white group of 100 swollen to 1,000, the riot had spread to the streets around the bus station. Freedom Riders who tried to flee were chased, knocked down and kicked. One Negro student was clubbed unconscious to the pavement with a baseball bat. The sight so enraged one local Montgomery Negro, a burly bricklayer, that he plowed into the melee and cried, "If you want to hit somebody, try me." Instantly, he too was knocked down. The bricklayer might very well have been killed if Floyd H. Mann, Alabama's director of public safety, had not arrived at that moment and taken a stance over his body with a drawn revolver.

"We'll not have any killings on these streets," roared Mann.

Fully fifteen minutes—witnesses agreed later—had elapsed since the riot began, and only now were state troopers and, more importantly, the city police arriving. This despite the fact that Montgomery authorities had been warned by the FBI that the bus was coming and police cruisers had trailed it from the outskirts of the city to the Montgomery bus station.* Ulti-

---

* The U.S. Commission on Civil Rights, in its 1961 report, cited the experience of the Freedom Riders as an example of "dereliction of duty by American police officers—condonation of or connivance in private violence."

mately, tear-gas bombs fired by the Montgomery police broke up the mob at the depot. But for the next two hours, bands of aroused whites roamed the downtown streets, attacking any Montgomery Negroes unlucky enough to be in the way. In all, twenty people were injured. And in a final fit of frenzy, angry whites at the bus station had seized the suitcases dropped by the Riders, banged them against the depot walls until clothing and books flew out and then set fire to the contents.

This happened on May 20, 1961, at the end of the first week of the Freedom Rides. Conceived, organized and led by James Farmer, the national director of CORE, the Freedom Rides were a daring extension of the new theory of direct mass action —or, more simply, demonstrations—then coming into prominence. The spring of 1960 had seen the first great wave of demonstrations: the sit-ins at restaurants and lunch counters in which an estimated 70,000 Negroes and whites took part in 100 cities of the South and of several border states as well. Then James Farmer decided to challenge segregation in interstate bus terminals by having Negroes boldly ride in and use white facilities. This kind of direct confrontation inflamed many Southern whites. "I cannot guarantee protection for this bunch of rabble-rousers," cried Governor John Patterson of Alabama.

Nor did he, very much. Having departed Washington, D.C., on May 4, the Freedom Riders proceeded southward more or less without incident until they reached Alabama. Just outside Anniston, Alabama, on May 14, a mob of whites set upon one of the buses and burned it into a twisted mass of blackened steel. The same day a second bus was stopped at Birmingham, and several of the Riders were beaten. And then fresh new Riders sprang forward to take up the cause and to ride into a hail of fists and baseball bats on that somber May 20 in Montgomery.

As far as the Negroes are concerned, the essential ingredient of their demonstrations has been nonviolence. Those who took part in the sit-ins and later the Freedom Rides were all rigorously schooled to take what came their way and never hit back, but not to be afraid and, more than that, to love those who were attacking them. Louis Lomax, in *The Negro Revolt,* speaks of this as a "new religion," a blend of Confucius, Moses, Jesus, Gandhi and Thoreau, yet uniquely the American Negro's own.

That bloody week of May 1961 presented the sternest test up until then of the new religion. It was then that the nation realized how determined the Negro really was. And it was then that the Negro himself was tempered and steeled for the battles still to come. Today, most Negroes are convinced that these demonstrations were the torch that set the smoldering civil-rights battle ablaze. In their view, the sit-ins and the sit-downs, the pickets and the marchers and the riders awakened white America to the real plight of the Negro and showed that the black man at last meant business. Indeed, the demonstrations had just about the same effect on the Negro himself. It was as if, after so many years of submission, the Negro suddenly discovered that he had a collective purpose and a collective courage and, what was more, the collective power to make the white man take notice of, and even yield to, his wants. Although to a small minority of Negroes the demonstrations had merely stirred up trouble and very possibly had set the Negro cause back—by stiffening the attitude of the whites—to the vast majority (80 per cent) they were an exhilarating exercise in racial pride and accomplishment. When the Negroes were asked in the poll "What effect do you feel the demonstrations of Negroes all over the country have had up to now?" these were typical responses of the majority from the rank and file:

"A tremendous effect—they have let the white American realize we are tired of their complacency, tired of being free in word for a hundred years and then suffered so much abuse and inequity"—Mrs. John Stone of Houston, Texas.

"Got the white folks shaking"—an unemployed Chicagoan.

"They have made the white man stop and look, for he thought the Negro did not have it in him to fight"—a truck driver's wife, aged 40, of Brooklyn, New York.

"Demonstrating gives other Negroes the urge to do something. It's like a fever—it's catching"—Mrs. Mary Cook of Chicago, Illinois.

"It showed those whites we ain't gonna take that stuff no more"—a postal clerk's wife in Philadelphia, Pennsylvania.

The leadership group was also very enthusiastic about the demonstrations. Nevertheless, when it comes to defining the effect they have had, one difference between the rank and file and the leadership should be noted. Many more rank-and-file Negroes (40 per cent) than leaders (24 per cent) think of the demonstrations in strongly positive terms—of getting results or showing the whites that they mean business. Among the majority of leaders (63 per cent) the prevailing—and much more cautious—tendency is to think of the demonstrations as a means of bringing the plight of the Negroes to the attention of the country. Only 18 per cent of the rank and file emphasized this effect.

Even so, the demonstrations obviously have had an inspiring effect on all Negroes. This is thrown into sharper focus when we examine the response to two companion questions in the poll.

In the first, each Negro was asked if he or any member of his family had already been out taking part in civil-rights activities. A fair number of rank-and-file Negroes, it turned out, already had demonstrated, and among the leaders—even though, as we have seen, the leaders are more cautious in how they assess the value of the demonstrations—the degree of participation was five times as great. More than half of the leaders, or members of their families, already had marched or picketed, and one in five had actually gone to jail. Added up in table form, this is how the participation of the Negro looks:

NEGRO PARTICIPATION IN DIRECT ACTION

	Rank and File %	Leaders %
Marched in demonstration	12	62
Picketed a store	9	54
Taken part in a sit-in	8	39
Gone to jail	4	21

Contrast this now with the next question, which was: *If asked,* would you do these things? Here the potential involvement of the Negroes soared by leaps and bounds. Among the rank and file, roughly half—and that's almost 10 million people—were willing to participate in such actions, a figure that put them much closer to the leadership:

NEGRO WILLINGNESS TO PARTICIPATE

	Rank and File %	Leaders %
March in demonstration	51	57
Take part in a sit-in	49	57
Go to jail	47	58
Picket a store	46	57

Thus it can be seen that some 10 million Negroes stand ready to assert their rights. Their resolve gives the lie to those Southern whites who have maintained that only a handful of "rabble-rousers" among the Negroes really want equal rights. In actuality, this social revolution is very broadly based and very deep-seated among the ranks of Negroes in America. It is a rather remarkable revolution, too, in that it defies the Puritan ethic and respect for convention that survives in this country. At no other time in American history have so many people gone peaceably into the streets to espouse a cause—in defiance often of local laws and in defiance also of the Puritan notion that going to jail is somehow a disgrace. For a great many Negroes, obviously, going to jail is no longer a shameful blot on their record; it has become a badge of honor.

The ambush slaying of Negro leader Medgar Evers at Jackson, Mississippi, in 1963, and the spectacle of police dogs and fire hoses used against Negro marchers in Birmingham, Alabama, in the same year, had much to do with rallying Negroes as well as white supporters to the cause.* Quite a few comments volunteered by Negroes in the survey indicated that these incidents had made them want to join in the fight. Many others, however, said they simply could not stand idly by while others of their

* Dogs had been used before, in Greenwood, Miss., but their appearance in Birmingham received more emphasis because more people were involved there and because some striking news photographs of the event received wide publicity.

race carried on the struggle. These were typical observations, from both the rank and file and the leadership:

"The Negro is waking up and so am I"—a young engine mechanic of Memphis, Tennessee.

"You get the spirit when you see terrible things happening to others"—a woman stockroom supervisor in Atlanta, Georgia.

"There was a time I didn't know whether I could take the abuse. Now I know I can because I have been abused. Abuse has encouraged me to do more"—Mrs. Della Mitchell, a CORE leader of High Point, North Carolina.

"I wouldn't feel it was a disgrace for me to go to jail now as I once would. Once I thought it was a disgrace to get involved. Now I feel it's a disgrace not to get involved"—Rev. Marshall L. Shepard, Philadelphia city councilman.

This kind of sentiment, the survey clearly showed, has instilled in the Negroes an unmistakable sense of urgency, a strong desire to get on with the fight. A clear majority of 72 per cent of the Negroes queried made it clear that they personally felt they had been pushed around long enough and were prepared to "go for broke."

They cited a variety of reasons for the sense of urgency. Some noted that 1963 marked the 100th anniversary of the Emancipation Proclamation and felt that this had somehow spurred the Negro into action. Others believed that the example of the emerging black nations of Africa inspired the American Negro to take up his own cause. Still others felt that the depressing effect of automation on Negro employment and his general economic plight in an era of high prices and high taxes drove him to seek relief. Another view was that a younger and more impatient generation of Negroes has taken over from a passive older generation. The most common reason voiced by the Negroes, however, and one on which they are quite vehement, is that they are simply sick and tired of waiting any longer for their rights, now that they have sensed these rights are within reach. Cecil Moore, the militant NAACP leader in Philadelphia, exclaimed, "My definition of now is yesterday." Comedian Dick Gregory, who has gone to jail in the revolution, commented, "The Constitution guarantees the rights I was born with. They are long overdue." And in Lumberton, North Carolina, a doctor's receptionist said, "It has been nine years since the Supreme Court ruled and it doesn't take nine years to do nothing unless you don't intend to."

Although the public demonstrations have dominated the headlines in recent years, the Negroes have been using another powerful weapon in their fight for equal rights. This is the boycott. The use of this weapon goes back as far as December 1955, when Mrs. Rosa Parks, a seamstress weary from her day's work, refused to give up her bus seat to a white in Montgomery, Alabama. Mrs. Parks was arrested, and from her defiance sprang the massive Montgomery bus boycott (some authorities date the actual birth of the Negro revolution from this incident). Led by Martin Luther King, Jr., and several dozen ministers of the Montgomery Improvement Association, some 17,000 Negroes—who made up three-fourths of the Montgomery bus line's customers—shunned the buses for more than a year, walking or riding in car pools to work. They endured harassment and violence, but in the end they won decisions in the Federal District Court and before the U.S. Supreme Court, and segregation on the buses in Montgomery ended. It has been estimated that the Montgomery boycott cost the bus company $750,000 in lost revenues. The Montgomery boycott led to similar efforts elsewhere—not all of them successful. It also led to a less visible kind of economic sanction: the refusal to patronize stores that practice discrimination, and the refusal to buy products made by companies which discriminate.

The survey revealed that 33 per cent of rank-and-file Negroes and a strong 69 per cent of the Negro leaders have boycotted certain stores in their towns. The degree of participation is smallest among low-income Negroes of the North (6 per cent), who very probably do not have the means to shop around, or who may not be sophisticated enough to realize the power they hold in their dollars. Similarly, 16 per cent of the rank and file and 52 per cent of the leaders said they have boycotted the products of companies that discriminate against Negroes. The victims of the boycotts generally have been certain popular breads, dairy products, beer and soft drinks, as well as the better-known dime-store chains. One NAACP leader in Atlanta, Georgia, Mrs. Ruby Hurley, reported that she had bought nothing in Atlanta for three years, but maintained charge accounts in New York stores and ordered by mail.

The survey showed that boycotting largely is spread by word of mouth or from the pulpits of the Negro churches. Not all Negroes are aware themselves of what stores or companies practice discrimination, but they don't have to be. Word from the grapevine is all many of them need to steer them away from a certain store or a certain product. There is enormous potential in the boycott, and Negro leaders are at last beginning to understand how well the dollar can be used as a lever in the civil-rights struggle. Although they often receive the lowest wages, collectively the Negroes of America pour some $20 billion a year into the nation's economy for goods and services. While not too many Negroes have boycotted as yet, a hefty 62 per cent of them—and that's more than 11 million—said they stand ready to boycott if they are asked by their leaders to do so in the cause of civil rights.

We have seen, thus far, that the Negro is nothing if not militant, and he is fully prepared to use the weapons at his command to get what he wants. But does he recognize the dangers inherent in his continuing fight, and just how far is he prepared to go? Apparently he does recognize the danger, and he is, by and large, prepared to go as far as it takes to win his rights. In the poll, the Negroes were asked this question: "What are the dangers, if any, in the demonstrations?" By an overwhelming 74 per cent, they recognized that the consequences could well be more bloodshed and riot, police brutality, injury and even death. Here again it was evident that the police dogs and fire hoses of Birmingham had done much to awaken the Negroes, for many said it was these that convinced them their cause would not easily be won. The Negroes have long contended that it is the whites who have started the violence, but some now recognize that continued demonstrations might also provoke violence on the part of the Negroes. Some also seem to feel that the potential for violence lies chiefly in the South and will not be much of a factor in the North (despite the fact that the city of Chicago was torn by repeated housing strife during the summer of 1963). These were typical comments from the rank and file and the leadership on the subject of danger:

"There will be plenty of fights and even people getting killed. The white man has to let his hate off somewhere"—a 68-year-old pensioner of Miami, Florida.

"There will be trouble in the South. The Southern white man is still fighting the Civil War"—a Cleveland, Ohio, housewife.

"Of course there will be violence. Do you know that there are Southerners that would rather see you dead than win? That's why I hate them today"—Mrs. Mildred D. Wall of Washington, D.C.

"We always have faced danger. Being a Negro has been dangerous to start with. We have been beat and lynched and killed anyway"—an auto factory worker of Detroit, Michigan.

"There will be some violence by misguided people on both sides, white and Negro"—A. M. Carter, an Augusta, Georgia, businessman.

"Danger for the white people. They're the ones who need to be careful. [The Negroes] may start to lynch white people soon." —an unemployed man in Chicago.

"Medgar Evers was only one casualty in a war which tragically continues and will intensify as further crises arise. There will be more casualties, both black and white—these are inevitable in a conflict of this kind. There are many Negroes, both those actively participating in the civil rights revolution and others who would appear to be quiescent, who are prepared to endure danger, physical pain, even death, if necessary."— Allan Morrison, New York journalist.

Despite their awareness of the dangers involved, the Negroes maintain an underlying hope that they can avoid bloodshed. This is shown graphically in their answers to the question, Do you personally feel Negroes today can win their rights without resorting to violence or do you think it will have to be an eye for an eye and a tooth for a tooth? Here are the results:

THE ROAD AHEAD: VIOLENT OR NONVIOLENT?

	Low-Income Non-South %	Total Rank and File %	Leaders %
Nonviolent	50	63	93
Violent	25	22	4
Not sure	25	15	3

Nearly two-thirds of the rank and file and almost all of the leaders are pinning their hopes on nonviolence. But in many ways the most significant response to this question is the 22 per cent of rank-and-file Negroes and the 25 per cent of non-South slum dwellers who think that some violence is inevitable. Throughout the civil-rights struggle the Negro leaders have been dedicated to nonviolence, but clearly a sizable number of their followers, roughly five million, are resigned to the possibility that they may have to fight their way to freedom.

Among those who rely on nonviolence to win the day there was substantial agreement that the Negro can never really win and live peaceably with the white man afterward if he resorts to the tactics of violence. For instance, the Rev. Ralph David Abernathy of the Southern Christian Leadership Conference, who has fought many a nonviolent battle himself, observed: "An eye-for-an-eye and tooth-for-a-tooth philosophy will eventually end up with a blind and toothless society." Here, some Negroes also distinguish between violence inflicted on them by the whites and retaliation in kind. As Cecil Moore, Philadelphia's NAACP leader, put it, "In every one of our demonstrations, the other parties have gotten violent." An 18-year-old unemployed youth in Selma, North Carolina, expressed the recurrent feeling that if there was widespread bloodshed, it would be because of white intransigence. "These white folks are hard to convince. It's going to take some violence."

But the most striking aspect of the answers to the question on whether violence is inevitable remains the difference between the leadership and the rank-and-file Negroes—particularly those in the Northern slums. This cleavage is thrown into sharper relief when we look at the answers to a companion question which was phrased thus: Some people have said that since there are ten whites for every Negro in America, if it came to white against Negro, the Negroes would lose. Do you agree with this or disagree?

SHOWDOWN WITH WHITES: WHO WOULD WIN

	Low-Income Non-South %	Total Rank and File %	Leaders %
Negroes would lose	25	20	54
Negroes would not lose	62	52	29
Not sure	13	28	17

It was on this question that the comments of the Negroes were perhaps the most interesting. More than half of the Negro leaders by and large thought their race could not win. They offered the perfectly reasonable explanation that, after all, the Negroes *are* outnumbered by the whites and hence can hardly expect to win. Besides, the leaders pointed out, the whites have all the weapons on their side—the Army and the Navy and the Air Force—as well as control of the police departments. Taking the long view, some leaders also felt that if relations between the races ever come to a point where there is an open clash, then neither side could really win, and democracy itself would be the loser.

But rank-and-file Negroes, and most especially the slum dwellers outside the South, do not see it that way. In almost reverse proportion they are convinced they could win, no matter what the odds are against them. Notice also, in the "not sure" results, that the slum dwellers have the least doubts of all about their ability to handle the whites. This, combined with the 25 per cent of low-income Northern Negroes who thought some violence is inevitable, suggests that the gravest threat of bloodshed seems to be in the big cities—it is there that the dynamite is stored. Furthermore, when the willingness of many Negroes to demonstrate and to go to jail is coupled with their feeling that they can win any real test, it is plain that the Birmingham riots of 1963 could be duplicated in almost any large city. Incidentally, a curious fact to emerge from the poll is that fully 6 per cent of all Negroes—more than one million of them—just do not believe that whites outnumber Negroes in the United States by ten to one. The only obvious explanation for this would seem to be that these Negroes are simply not familiar with the population statistics or find them hard to believe—living as they do in all-black ghettos.

From another viewpoint, the fact that 10 million or more Negroes were convinced their side could win has a different meaning. For here emerged the Negro's fundamental faith in his own worth—his yearning belief that he is as good as, or better than, the white any day. He may be downtrodden, said the Negro in effect, but he is a better street fighter, a better gut fighter, than the white. Just let him get his hands on the white in a fair, even fight, and he was certain to win. A machine operator's wife in St. Louis summed up this sentiment very well when she commented, "Hell, now, you give a Negro a good sharp knife and he can get him ten whites any day." A 36-year-old man who does odd jobs in Jackson, Mississippi, agreed: "I think I can handle ten of them myself." And in Mt. Vernon, New York, William Albert Jones said, "The white man hasn't the heart that the Negroes have. The white man faints at the sight of blood."

Louis Lomax has written that the rising revolution of 1963 sprang from the "total collapse of the Negro's faith in the basic integrity of the white power structure." This may well be true, insofar as the deepest motivation of the revolt is concerned. Very probably the Negroes *were* driven into the streets by final disenchantment with the notion that white leaders would eventually see the justice of their cause and give them their rights. Yet the Negroes also seem to recognize that the social revolution they have embarked on cannot really succeed ultimately without the tolerance of the white man himself and the aid of white institutions. For example, despite the success of the demonstrations and their dramatic effect on morale, not all Negroes are convinced that demonstrations will continue to be the answer to everything. When it comes to equal treatment in such places as restaurants, movie theaters and hotels and motels, many (39 per cent) said they would rather have a public-accommodations provision from a white Congress, which was a major object of their 1963 march on Washington. Still more (41 per cent) said they would rather see their leaders sit down with the whites and work out an agreement.

When they look to white institutions for help, the Negroes put less faith in Congress than they do in both the Executive branch of the government, headed by the President, and the courts. But there is a sharp split between the rank and file and the leadership as to which of the two they trust more. By 44 per cent, the rank and file favor the Executive branch, while 59 per cent of the leaders look to the courts. The explanation for the disparity seems to be that the Negro leaders are inclined to put their trust in the solid substance of judicial dicta, while the rank and file—perhaps because of unfamiliarity with the courts or more likely for emotional reasons—tend to look to the President for the fulfillment of their hopes—at least they did when President Kennedy was alive.

The viewpoint of the leaders was well expressed by Harvey N. Schmidt, a Philadelphia attorney, who said, "The Supreme Court is a continuing body whose influence will make itself felt through and beyond many Presidents. Of course a President can do much, but a succeeding President can undo his acts. The court's decision will have a much more lasting effect."

In his struggle to break out of his bondage, the Negro, we have seen, is impatient and he is militant, sometimes more so than his leaders. He is dedicated to a course of nonviolence, but he is not afraid of violence if it comes. Ultimately he expects to need the help of the white man, but in the meantime he is using every lever, every wedge, and every weapon at his command to further his own cause.

There are, however, two other spearheads that are of the foremost importance to his fight. One is his church. There can be no doubt that the Negro church has been a powerful force in the Negro revolution—as a spokesman, as a rallying point, as a sanctuary in time of trouble and as a primary source of a great many of the revolt's leaders. Coupled with this is the Negro's own strong religious faith—his firm belief that his cause is not only just under the law of the land but right before God.

The other spearhead is his politics. Politics has always been a classic weapon of revolutions, yet the American Negro has not always made good use of it; and we need to examine why and what may be his political course in the years ahead. Both of these instruments are of such importance, however, that they will be discussed in separate chapters.

CHAPTER 5

THE
POLITICS
OF RACE

THE MOST OUTSTANDING political fact about Negroes in America is that they constitute a largely nonvoting minority that nevertheless wields tremendous power and could wield infinitely more. Compared with any other 10 per cent in the population, fewer Negroes have registered to vote, fewer have come out on election day, fewer have held high office and fewer have been in the mainstream of the American political system.

Yet politicians of both major parties probably talk more about the Negro vote than about any other 10 per cent of the electorate. Only the much vaunted farm vote challenges the Negro vote in the nurture and care afforded it by professional politicos.

The reason is simple. Despite the Negro's relatively poor turnout at the polls, two out of the last three men elected President have candidly acknowledged that if it hadn't been for the votes of Negroes they probably never would have gained the White House. Both Presidents Truman and Kennedy won in "squeakers" where the Negro vote played a crucial role.

In 1964, Negroes once again find themselves in an important political position—especially in the key industrial states of the North. With John F. Kennedy in the White House, the Negroes were one of a coalition of minority groups which formed a bastion of Democratic big-city, big-state strength. With the tragic assassination of Kennedy in November of 1963, Democratic certainties of winning the industrial North were shaken. First, the late President from Massachusetts had extraordinary appeal in that area. Second, his successor, Lyndon Johnson, came from Texas: the first Southerner to serve as President in modern times. Whereas Kennedy's pulling power in the industrial North was proven in 1960, Johnson's potential had yet to be tested. In view of this uncertainty, the Negro vote once again took on important proportions.

Negroes have thus created more of a stir in American politics with less over-all participation than any other comparable group. By the same token, at the time of the *Newsweek* poll, Negroes had probably received as little from the political system as any other group. Presidents, governors, mayors and, above all, congressmen and senators had long since acquired the habit of talking a lot about civil rights while doing little in terms of concrete action. In fact, the one arm of the Federal government most removed from politics— the Supreme Court—had undoubtedly been more effective than any of the others in pressing for Negro rights.

Yet in the surging Negro revolution of the 1960s, political action is surely a major weapon the Negroes must acquire. For, as many others have learned before them, effectiveness in elections is the surest route to power in American politics and government. And if Negroes want the full support of the Federal government, they will have to find the political muscle to back up their demands.

As the Rev. Martin Luther King, Jr., said, "The constructive program ahead must include a campaign to get Negroes to register and vote. . . . Even where the polls are open to all, Negroes have shown themselves too slow to exercise their voting privileges. There must be a concerted effort on the part of Negro leaders to arouse their people from their apathetic indifference to this obligation of citizenship. In the past, apathy was a moral failure. Today, it is a form of moral and political suicide."

So far, it has been only in very close elections—in 1948 and in 1960—that Negroes have played a pivotal role in deciding who would occupy the White House. But if the Negroes want continuing and effective political power, they must demonstrate their strength more than every 12 years. It is perhaps not understating the case to say that the single greatest challenge to Negro leadership is to realize the political potential of the Negro at the polls. In other words, how to get the Negro registered? And how to get him to vote?

The reason why the significant Negro vote potential has not been realized to date was an important area of inquiry in the poll. Two others were: which party and which candidates would Negroes support, and what would be the future of Negro political action? The poll results, however, must be viewed in the light of certain background facts.

Up to 1964 the political effectiveness of the Negro vote has been confined almost entirely to a relatively small number of Negroes in seven pivotal, industrial states: New York, Pennsylvania, New Jersey, Ohio, Michigan, Illinois and California. Exactly one-third of all Negroes in the country live in these seven states, which together contribute 212 electoral votes out of the magic 268 needed to win the Presidency. No candidate for President in modern times has won without taking a substantial share of the votes of the big seven. Rarely does any one of these states vary more than two or three percentage points from the national division of votes for the two Presidential candidates; when the voting is close on a nationwide basis the vote in the seven industrial states is also close. And under our electoral-college system, all a candidate for President has to do is to win the state by one vote to collect all the electoral votes of that state.

This being the case, the first fact of political life for the Negroes in the 1960s is that they have the good fortune of living under the electoral-college system and in addition find their numbers concentrated in the big cities of the states which are pivotal under that system. This concentration gives Negroes added political effectiveness, particularly when the white vote is split down the middle. When that happens the Negroes can move in and elect a President. The 1960 election was a prime example. In that year, if the decision had been up to the 92 per cent of the electorate made up of whites, Richard Nixon would occupy the White House today, for he carried the white vote by a 52-48 per cent margin. However, Mr. Kennedy did so well among Negroes in 1960 (with fully 78 per cent of their vote) that he made up his white deficit and won by a narrow margin.

The 1960 role of Negroes in electing John F. Kennedy was indeed critical. But it is also important to bear in mind that both in 1952 and in 1956, Negroes also voted in rather heavy majorities for Democrat Adlai E. Stevenson for President. Yet the Negro vote really didn't make any difference in the final outcome. President Eisenhower was able to find more than enough votes elsewhere, outside the Negro community, to win election by decisive margins.

This points up another political fact of life for Negroes in the 1960s. They can enhance their political importance by helping the Democrats win a close national election, for recent experience indicates that the Democrats *must* have a massive Negro vote to win elections. Conversely, when a Republican wins the White House, the Negroes lose bargaining power; for recent elections indicate that the Republicans would fare much better every four years if there were no Negro vote at all.

We have seen the power that can be wielded by the 33 per cent of Negroes who live in seven Northern industrial states. But what of the largest concentration of Negroes in this country—the 52 per cent who live in the 11 states of the old South? Potentially, if they all were registered, the Negroes in the South could amass a total of 5,184,000 votes. However, in the early 1960s only about 1,600,000 Southern Negroes were registered, a scant 30 per cent. The vast majority—seven out of every ten Negroes in the South—had either been deprived of their vote or had failed to exercise their franchise out of fear or apathy. While an actual majority of Negroes may live in the South, the overwhelming preponderance of voting Negroes is outside the South, as the following table indicates:

NEGRO POPULATION VS. NEGRO VOTING

	Distribution of Negro Population %	Negro Vote %
South	52	38
Non-South	48	62

Here the political problem for Negroes is clearly spelled out. Obviously, the Northern minority of the Negro people is carrying the main political burden. Even so, surveys have indicated that while an estimated 72 per cent of the white voters in the North came out to vote in 1960, only 55 per cent of their Negro counterparts were able—or willing—to vote. But that 55 per cent was enough to make Senator Kennedy President.

In the South, the potential Negro vote is so vast that it could change the political map. The table on page 83—drawn from registration figures and state polls—graphically illustrates this fact.

The disparity between Negro population and Negro voting is obviously massive. But just as the concentration of Negroes in seven Northern states has given them enormous political leverage, their concentration in the South gives them enormous

POTENTIAL NEGRO VOTE IN THE SOUTH

	Per Cent in Population	Per Cent of Registered Voters	Eligible Unregistered Negroes
Mississippi	42	7	396,000
South Carolina	35	8	358,000
Louisiana	32	14	356,000
Alabama	30	5	415,000
Georgia	28	6	454,000
North Carolina	24	10	340,000
Arkansas	22	12	120,000
Virginia	21	9	340,000
Florida	18	9	287,000
Tennessee	17	8	179,000
Texas	12	7	338,000
		Total:	3,583,000

political potential. If Negroes in the past four years, for example, had been able to register only two in ten of their present unregistered numbers in the South, and if these newly registered Negroes had voted against extreme segregationists in the Democratic primaries, then Governor Paul Johnson would have been defeated in Mississippi, Governor George Wallace would have lost in Alabama, Orval Faubus might not be Governor of Arkansas, Governor Farris Bryant would have been out in Florida and Governor Jimmie Davis would have lost in Louisiana. Assuming that the division of the white vote remained constant, the most outspoken opponents of integration in the state houses of the South could have been defeated in one fell swoop.

But this is mere potential. Negroes have to pass a number of thresholds first. The *Newsweek* poll cast light on these in human terms as it probed Negro experience and intentions on the first threshold that must be crossed: registering to vote.

The cross-section of Negroes was asked how long ago they first registered to vote. For the country as a whole, it was found that eligible Negroes were registering at the rate of 4 per cent a year. Significantly, however, the rate in the South was double that outside the South. In concrete terms, this means that roughly 300,000 Negroes are being registered every year now in the South. If this rate were to continue for another five years, the number of Negroes voting in the South would double. But there would still be more than two million unregistered, and although registration would have increased greatly in some southern states, it would still be very low in the Deep South.

The process of getting Negroes registered is long, laborious and sometimes perilous. Among those who have never registered or voted, the poll probed to find out why they had not:

WHY NEGROES HAVEN'T REGISTERED

	Total Rank and File %	Total South %
Just haven't got around to it	64	64
Not qualified (residency, education)	13	2
Election officials wouldn't allow	6	11
Can't be effective in voting, politics	6	7
Don't believe in voting	5	10
Can't pay poll tax	2	4
Illness	4	2

Almost two out of every three unregistered Negroes seemed to be victims of what Martin Luther King called "the suicide of apathy." A 30-year-old housewife from Riviera Beach, Florida, was frank in admitting this: "I'm just lazy, that's all." Among the rest, there is a sense of discouragement, a feeling that the authorities, especially those in the South, will bend every effort to keep them from registering. Typical was a 44-year-old woman in Sumter, South Carolina, who said, "I wouldn't even try. The white man has the law in his hands." James E. Davis, 22, of Montgomery, Alabama, was convinced "it was pretty hard to get the application blank to fill out."

The fears of those who had not tried to register were quickly confirmed by Negroes who reported they had tried to register. The following table sums up the experience of those who say they went down to register but were unsuccessful:

WHY NEGROES WHO TRIED
TO REGISTER WERE NOT ABLE TO

	Nationwide %
Turned back, threatened by authorities	33
Papers not in order	19
Lacked education requirements	15
Asked questions until finally couldn't answer	14
Couldn't pay poll tax	14
Whites kept getting in line ahead of me	5

Most humiliating and frightening to Negroes was their treatment at the hands of authorities. Many reported that they had been threatened or had experienced actual violence. A bricklayer from Woodville, Mississippi, reflected this when he said, "We were afraid to try to vote." And a 77-year-old man in Montgomery, Alabama, reported, "They tore up my paper when I first tried to get an application." A 29-year-old painter from Jackson, Mississippi, described his problem this way: "You had to pay a white guy so they'd let you register. But if you tried it, then you were threatened [for offering him money]." And a 57-year-old housewife in Union Spring, Alabama, told of the retribution wrought on her husband when she took the trouble to register: "My husband was fired off his job because I registered to vote. He does not vote." A 22-year-old truck driver in Jackson, Mississippi, told of outright violence: "Some of my friends got beat up when they tried."

Especially degrading, many Negroes reported, was the relentless questioning at the polls. A truck loader in Birmingham, Alabama, reported, "They asked so many questions till I couldn't answer them and I just got fainthearted and just haven't went back." Or in the words of a 36-year-old housemaid in Jackson, Mississippi, "They say I didn't pass the part on the Constitution." This was echoed by a 54-year-old unemployed man in Woodville, Mississippi, who said, "I was disqualified because I did not satisfactorily interpret the constitution of the state of Mississippi."

Such tactics, especially those of intimidation, could, of course, be in violation of the Civil Rights Act of 1957, which bars any person from interfering by threats or coercion with any citizen's right to vote for Federal candidates. But proof is hard to establish. Up to the middle of 1963, only 41 cases had been filed under this law, and the whole process of enforcement in this area has been slow and bogged down in the courts. However, the filing of such suits in Federal courts has had the effect of triggering increased Negro registration. This happened in Macon County, Georgia, where registration more than tripled, from roughly 1,000 to 3,000, after such a complaint was filed, and in Bullock County in Alabama, where the number of Negroes registered rose from 5 to roughly 1,100, according to *Congressional Quarterly* reports.

While efforts to register Negroes still remain a promise rather than fulfillment, certainly increases in registration among Negroes are at this point outstripping those for whites. But the distance to be closed is great. What is more, if Negroes hope to achieve the political power implicit in their revolution, they will have to register people at a rate well beyond the present 4 per cent a year.

Increased Federal pressures should help break the log jam in the South. An aggressive Department of Justice will probably encourage higher Negro registration. And history is at work, as well. In the past, the impediments imposed on Negroes, coupled with apathy, could keep 70 per cent of all Negroes from voting in the South. Today, there is evidence that the efforts at intimidation and coercion are likely to be a powerful force for eliminating apathy. For the singular mark of this Negro revolution is that where white pressures become excessive, then Negroes actively want to join in nonviolent battle.

Over the last three Presidential elections, the Negro vote in America has gone no less than 2 to 1 Democratic. In 1952, when Dwight D. Eisenhower was breaking the long Democratic hold on the White House, the Negro vote went to Adlai Stevenson by a solid 75-25 per cent count. But four years later, Stevenson slipped to a 67-33 per cent margin. In 1960, the Democratic candidate, John F. Kennedy, soared back to better than normal majorities among Negroes, winning their vote by a 78-22 per cent margin.

So it certainly is no startling news that the Negroes are rather firmly wedded to the Democratic Party nationally. In the poll, more than ample confirmation of this fact could be found in both the North and the South. For example, it was found that among those registered to vote, 74 per cent consider themselves Democrats, 11 per cent Republicans, 14 per cent Independents and 1 per cent associate themselves with splinter parties. Furthermore, there is no substantial difference in the pattern North or South.

This monolithic pattern of pro-Democratic sentiment was broken among only one key group: the 100 leaders of the Negro community whom *Newsweek* interviewed. Among the leadership, a full 20 per cent consider themselves Republicans, and 25 per cent are Independents. Only 55 per cent of the leaders are regular Democrats.

It took little probing among the leaders to find out why they are less committed to the Democratic Party. So Dolores Branche of Chicago spoke for a number of the leaders when she said, "Democrats feel they have the Negro vote and I would like to have them less sure of our vote." And in Cleveland, Mississippi, the Rev. James L. Bevel didn't think the Negroes should ally themselves with either particular party at this time "because neither party has proven to be the ally of the Negro people. They should stay out and support the party with the best platform. Otherwise we can have no real political power as a group."

The key point, of course, is that if the Negroes are wholly and irrevocably committed to the Democratic Party—even if they do help win close elections—they will have pitifully little bargaining strength to enforce their demands on Democratic leadership. Intuitively—and quite sensibly—Negro leadership feels that any party in power tends to pay more attention to the votes of blocs they may *not* have than to those they feel they already have locked up.

But what are the leaders to do? With the Negro rank and file so firmly committed to the Democratic Party, the leadership is left little room for maneuver between the two parties. If the leaders flirt with the Republican Party, they might find a responsive moderate and liberal wing of the GOP ready to adopt an all-out pro-Negro position on civil rights. But if the Republicans ask in return substantial support at the polls from Negroes, the leaders could well find themseves in the embarrassing position of having delivered themselves but not their followers. In 1960, former baseball star Jackie Robinson vigorously supported Richard Nixon, only to find the day after election that he had delivered few Negroes other than himself to the Republican column.

Another classic demonstration of how a leader can be "locked in" by his followers was the case of John L. Lewis in the 1940 Presidential election. Then head of the CIO labor organization, Lewis bolted from the ranks of Franklin D. Roosevelt, threatening to lead labor away from the Democratic Party. Lewis' own membership stuck solidly with Roosevelt, allowing Lewis to deliver only himself and perhaps his immediate family to Republican candidate Wendell L. Willkie.

In one sense, the Democratic bias of the Negroes is something of an anomaly. Every February 12 on the anniversary of the Great Emancipator's death, Republican orators make much of the fact that it was the first GOP President, Abraham Lincoln, who fought the Civil War and set the slaves free. They can also point to the Congressional committee chairmanships to prove the powerful hold that segregationist Southern Democrats have on the Federal government. All during the period when the Supreme Court and the Federal judiciary were laying the groundwork for the Negro revolution, the chairman of the Senate Judiciary Committee—the body that had to pass on all Federal court appointments—was Senator James O. Eastland, an outspoken segregationist from Mississippi. Eastland is the direct product of the Democratic Senate seniority system.

It could be claimed that the Republican Party of Senators Case of New Jersey, Kuchel of California and Javits of New York is directly descended from Abraham Lincoln. It could also be claimed that the Democratic Party of Senators Harry

Byrd of Virginia, Eastland of Mississippi and Russell of Georgia among others, is the heir of the Democratic Party that fought Lincoln over the Civil War and has remained essentially pro-segregationist. Yet the Republican Party has steadily lost ground among Negroes, and even on a straight-out party test receives a vote of almost no confidence from the rank and file. The Negro cross-section in the poll was asked directly which party, the Democrats or the Republicans, will do more for Negro rights in the next few years. Only four out of every 100 people could bring themselves to believe in the Republican Party. To be sure, fully a third felt there was little or no difference between the two parties. But a solid majority of 63 per cent expressed confidence in the Democratic Party.

What is more, almost invariably when these Negroes express their praise for the Democratic Party, they add a dig at the Republican Party by way of contrast. For example, Mrs. Juanita Colbert, 43, a housewife from Oklahoma City, Oklahoma, was categorical about it: "The Democrat Party raises wages and makes it possible for everyone to live on a higher level. The Republican Party lowers wages." And Cleveland J. Peete, Sr., a housing-project manager in New Orleans, pointed out: "In the past years with Democrats in power, the Negro's economic condition has risen considerably. The Democrats work for the masses, the Republicans for the major industrial people, the bosses." A 39-year-old foundry worker from Cincinnati told us, "Republicans won't do anything. Republicans are rich." There are the rare exceptions, to be sure. Jesse Heath, 78, of Providence, Rhode Island, was one of them. "Remember," he said, "a Republican President ordered the troops at Little Rock."

As these comments reveal, most Negroes look on themselves as poorer people and on the Democratic Party as the friend of the underprivileged. This began with Roosevelt, continued with Truman and reached new heights under Kennedy. In John F. Kennedy, in fact, the Negroes found a new white champion. As a 27-year-old Washington, D.C., housewife said exuberantly, "I call him Mr. Wonderful." But Kennedy's popularity at his death was not entirely of his own doing. In large part it goes back to the emergence of the Democratic Party as the "champion of the underdog" under Franklin D. Roosevelt.

Detroit Negro leader Albert B. Cleage, Jr., remembers it well. "Roosevelt changed the tempo for the Negro struggle, gave the Negro a sense of being a participating part of American life. He recognized the political power of Negroes. He put together the Democratic Party which was made of basic elements in American life—the Negro was one of them. Negroes have built on this." The affection for Roosevelt runs deep among the rank and file as well. For instance, a retired factory worker from Detroit recalls, "He [Roosevelt] fixed it so we could draw pensions. He made a strong platform for civil rights. He brought light to us so that we would know we were human beings." And a widow from Cleveland said it for many middle-aged and older Negroes: "Roosevelt was sent by God."

On the subject of Harry S. Truman, Negroes register a marked ambivalence. Leaders rank him Number 2 among the past four Presidents as having done the most for their cause. Philadelphia leader Rev. Marshall L. Shepard summed up his opinion of all the last four Presidents when he said, "Roosevelt woke 'em up, Truman shook 'em up, Eisenhower held 'em up and Kennedy speeded 'em up." Then he added about Harry Truman, "Truman desegregated the Army, he sought to improve Negroes' working conditions through Fair Employment and sent troops here to get Negroes into the trolley cars. Truman did the most things you can put your hand on." But more than one out of three in the rank and file name him as having done the least—perhaps recalling some remarks made by Truman since he left the White House.

Which President, in the eyes of Negroes, has done the most for their cause? In the *Newsweek* poll taken four months before he was killed, Kennedy won in a runaway. Among the rank and file, 73 per cent singled out Kennedy, compared with 20 per cent who named Roosevelt, 4 per cent who named Eisenhower and 3 per cent who singled out Truman. On the negative side—which President did the least for Negro rights—Eisenhower headed the list, having been thus listed by 48 per cent of the rank and file.

The leadership showed considerably less enthusiasm for Kennedy than the rank and file, but he still was singled out by half the leadership group for the top position in helping Negro rights. General Eisenhower came off especially poorly with the leaders, emerging among 63 per cent as the President who had done the least for Negro rights. The criticism of the former Republican President was summed up by the Rev. A. K. Stanley, a Negro leader in ?reensboro, North Carolina, who said, "Though Eisenhower did some things, I was never sure he wanted anybody to know he did them."

The full measure of Negro support for President Kennedy was plumbed in another, more general question: What kind of job had he done as President? Eighty-nine per cent of the rank and file rated his over-all performance as "good to excellent." Among the more critical leadership group, Mr. Kennedy scored almost as well, recording an 82 per cent positive rating. At the time the survey was made, the President's standing with the country as a whole was hovering around the 60-40 per cent positive mark. Thus, Negro approval of Kennedy was running almost 30 percentage points higher than the rest of the country.

More than half the favorable comments about President Kennedy from these Negroes concerned his stand on behalf of civil rights. A 62-year-old laundry worker from Chicago commented thus: "He has done more for the Negroes than any President I know. He forced Wallace to get away from that door." Or as Mrs. Geraldine Robertson, 50, a Detroit housewife, said, "He has fortitude. He has courage. He is a God-fearing man and not man-fearing." A retired man from Pine Bluff, Arkansas, agreed: "He has done a lot to help the people. He stuck his neck out to help colored people."

Mrs. Johnnie Lane, a 29-year-old housewife from Miami, Florida, was quite specific and even personal: "President Kennedy put more Negroes in higher offices. He got the children into the previous all-white colleges and universities. He wants all public places to accept Negroes. His own child goes to an integrated kindergarten—that shows he practices what he preaches."

Others see the President's pro-Negro position as either a

response to the pressures brought upon him by the demonstration of Negro strength or motivated by his own political self-interest. A Detroit journalist, for example, expressed some signs of skepticism: "The President has only recently become aware of the Negro fight to achieve his rights. Prior to this, Kennedy genuinely felt that the Negro struggle would be assuaged by the appointment of a few Negroes to important positions in government." And Mrs. Lorraine Chavis, a 28-year-old housewife of Mt. Vernon, New York, was one of the minority still uncommitted to Kennedy: "He's not doing anything really. He's talking a lot but not writing his name on anything."

Such criticism, however, was more of the moment than lasting. There is little doubt that Negroes felt deeply the loss of John F. Kennedy. A. Philip Randolph said it for many, "The call of history in this hour of trial by fire is for Negroes in particular and America in general to march forward toward the goal of human dignity and social and racial justice, to honor this man whose place in history will be next to Abraham Lincoln—the greatest President this country has ever known."

The aftermath of the Kennedy assassination and the continuing upheaval of the Negro revolution could find American politics profoundly altered. As this book goes to press, the tragic killing of the President is still very recent, and the political history of 1964 remains to be written. The monolithic support for Kennedy by Negroes unquestionably provided an impetus to the candidacy of Senator Barry Goldwater. The philosophy behind his candidacy was to keep the conservative states of the North for the GOP and to add the Deep South as a clincher. This would come closer to putting together a genuine all-conservative coalition for the Republican Party than ever before. With Johnson, a Southerner, in the White House, the attractiveness of Goldwater's appeal diminished. Before Kennedy's death, moderates in the GOP also saw nothing but disaster and permanent minority status in the idea of forfeiting the pivotal industrial states. If President Kennedy had been the candidate, such an argument would have been rather academic,

for the GOP would have had only the slimmest chance of dent-
ing the Negro vote in 1964.

With Lyndon B. Johnson of Texas now in the White House,
both the monolithic nature of Negro support for the Democrats
and the implicit Republican admission that the GOP could win
among white people or not at all have been shaken. By taking
the same position as Kennedy on civil rights, Johnson will go
far toward keeping the vast majority of Negroes in the Democratic column. But whether he will approach the record Kennedy
level of support or will more nearly approximate the low-water
mark of Adlai Stevenson in 1956 will not be determined until
the 1964 election is close at hand. Traditionally, Negroes in
both North and South are suspicious of any politician who hails
from the South. The burden is upon President Johnson to prove
to Negroes that the words he speaks in behalf of Negro rights
will really be implemented in action. By the same token, Negro
demonstrations against Johnson will carry far more potential
damage than they could have had against Kennedy, whom Negroes revered and trusted, and who they felt had produced
under fire.

Compounding Johnson's problem is yet another problem,
deeply rooted in American political patterns. President Kennedy
at the time of his death was being hurt by a white back-lash to
the whole civil rights problem. A large white counter-reaction
to his pro-Negro sympathies was taking place. The whole history
of group voting in U.S. politics is that whenever one key segment veers overwhelmingly to one side, other elements tend to
back off from that side.

Precisely the opposite result could take place in the case of
Lyndon Johnson in 1964. Because he is likely to be *much*
stronger than Kennedy in the South, it is entirely possible that
Negro voters will eye with suspicion the support Johnson might
well receive from white segregationists in the South. It is perfectly apparent that both the Negro vote and the uncertainties
about it have mounted with Kennedy's death and Johnson's
accession to the White House.

In the surge of demonstrations that have marked the Negro

revolution, Negroes have depended primarily on Negroes to make their bid. To be sure, there is widespread recognition that support from whites is necessary, especially if the goal of integration is to be achieved. But there is a real question whether Negroes might not do better by organizing themselves as a separate political group and then throwing their weight where they can strike the most advantageous bargain for Negro rights. For many years, organized labor tried to pursue this policy, following the Samuel Gompers dictum of "rewarding labor's friends and punishing labor's enemies."

How do the Negroes feel about working as a separate political group as opposed to working within the established parties? According to the poll, the overwhelming sentiment (by better than 7 to 1) was for working within the existing parties —i.e., the Democratic Party.* Negroes feel this way partly because they believe political integration is no less important than any other form of integration. In short, any all-Negro political party would seem doomed to failure. As Dr. James M. Nabrit, Jr., president of Howard University, said, "We are not strong enough or wise enough to 'get' separately. Especially when we are trying to join the American society." Leader Edwin C. Berry of Chicago added, "It would be silly to form a separate structure contrary to all our goals of integration. I hope we're not forced into it."

The rank and file feel no less strongly. "We got to go into the party and work," said a pensioner in Miami, Florida. "It'll do more for the race. The Negroes can keep one eye on the white man and the other on each other." Or as a 58-year-old housewife from Miami said, "We're trying to get rid of discrimination and if we have it in our politics how can we tell other people how to live?" In the words of a 29-year-old laborer from St. Louis: "You can't do nothing with a divided house. We all have to work together to get what's right for everybody—

* Shortly after the *Newsweek* survey of Negroes was made, a national committee was formed to establish a new political party, called the Freedom Now Party, which would run Negro candidates on a pro-Negro-rights platform. Later, the National Civil Rights Party—also with a Negro slate—announced itself.

white and black." A 68-year-old man in Jackson, Mississippi, put it another way: "Any secondhand message you receive you don't get a straight message; so work together and get the message firsthand." And a welfare recipient in Washington, D.C., was looking well into the future when he said, "If we work together in the party, in this way, perhaps someday one of us could run for President."

The future of the Negro revolution depends in large part on how many Negroes will fight through the impediments to registration and how many will come to cast their ballots in every election from now on. Success in these two areas will determine whether or not the Negro's potential power—which could change the political map of North and South alike—is realized.

CHAPTER 6

THE ROLE
OF THE NEGRO
CHURCH

IN THE YEAR 1787 the white elders of St. George's Methodist Episcopal Church, on Fourth Street in Philadelphia, were sorely troubled. They had, the year before, invited a former Negro slave named Richard Allen to preach at the church because of his spellbinding powers as an orator. But Allen's eloquence attracted an ever-increasing number of Negro worshipers to St. George's—so many, in fact, that it seemed prudent to the elders to assign them segregated seats along the walls. And then one Sabbath morning Richard Allen himself, with several of his closest followers, came to worship and went boldly to the gallery reserved for whites. Allen wrote later that they did this because the church sexton had directed them to the gallery. But no matter. White men descended on the Allen group and wrenched them from their knees as they prayed. Richard Allen's answer was to stride out of St. George's and never return. With one of his companions, Absalom Jones, he set up a church of his own in a blacksmith shop, calling it the Free African Society. In 1816 he founded the African Methodist Episcopal Church, which is today one of the larger denominations of the Negro church in America.

There had been a few other Negro churches in early American history; the first known was a Baptist church founded at Silver Bluff, South Carolina, between the years 1773 and 1775. But they were scattered and mostly existed by sufferance of a few kindly slaveowners. Richard Allen's defiant departure from St. George's marked the beginning of the independent Negro church in America, an institution that was to grow to prodigious proportions through the years and become today one of the main sources of leadership in the Negro revolt.

During the Revolutionary War period, when feeling against the Negro was muted by the common cause of American freedom, he was allowed a measure of access to white churches, though very often in segregated pews, and it was not uncommon for Negro preachers (as in the case of Richard Allen) to speak in white churches. But later, as slavery tightened its hold on the young country, the Negro was wanted less and less in white churches. It was in this period that the church movement thrived. Sometimes, notably in the rural South, the Negro was encouraged by the whites to establish his own church. After all, they reasoned, religion was a harmless opiate as long as the Negro preacher stuck to other-worldly matters—and perhaps it could even be beneficial if the preacher counseled his flock to be good and faithful servants to their masters.

But for the slave Negro, his church was something that he desperately needed. It filled a great vacuum in his life of subjugation and despair. Denied any other kind of rights and considered by the whites to be subhuman, the Negro discovered in his church the only place where he could be a person. There he could at least find a brief surcease from slavery; there he could run his own affairs and worship as he pleased.

Indeed, the special role of the church in the Negro slave's life had much to do with the rituals and customs that survive in that church today. His need for an outlet for pent-up feelings helped give rise to services considerably more emotional than white services, marked by fervent gospel singing, audible approval of the preacher's words and, at times, what *The Christian Century* has called "bodily seizures." The Negro's need for some semblance of status, in a world where he otherwise had none, produced a high degree of lay participation with numerous singing groups of young and old and layer upon layer of church functionaries. Another very direct result was that unique contribution of the Negro church to American culture: the spiritual.

In his poetic story of the Negro spirituals, *Deep River*,* Howard Thurman writes that many were based on Bible stories with which the Negro could identify his own seemingly hopeless lot and his own longing for release. Thus, Daniel in the lion's den was a recurring theme; it emerged in one spiritual as follows:

> My Lord delivered Daniel,
> My Lord delivered Daniel,
> My Lord delivered Daniel,
> Why can't he deliver me?

Some of the Negro's most poignant songs expressed the conviction that when he reached the Promised Land he would escape the travails of his life on earth. The most famous of these goes in part:

> I got shoes,
> You got shoes,
> All God's children got shoes.
> When we get to Heaven
> We're goin' to put on our shoes
> An' shout all over God's Heaven.
> Heaven! Heaven!

* Harper & Brothers, New York, 1945, 1955.

It is hardly an accident that many of the songs of the Negro's twentieth-century revolution derive from the old spirituals and gospel refrains, containing as they do the element of protest. By now, of course, the Negro no longer is content to wait until he reaches Heaven for deliverance. In taking over those songs, the Negro preserved the ancient melodies and simply substituted new words to suit his now militant quest for freedom. One spiritual began with the words "When I'm in trouble, Lord, walk with me." This has now become "Down in the jailhouse, Lord, walk with me." One of the oldest Negro spirituals, which begins, "If you want to get to Heaven, do what Jesus says," has become, somewhat prosaically, "If you want to get your freedom, register and vote." The Negro's most popular "freedom song," "We Shall Overcome," is probably based on an old Baptist hymn which began:

> I'll overcome, I'll overcome,
> I'll overcome, someday.
> O-o-oh, if in my heart I do not yield,
> I'll overcome someday.

As chanted now by Negroes and their white supporters all over the land, this has become:

> We shall overcome, We shall overcome,
> We shall overcome, someday, someday.
> O-o-oh deep in my heart I do believe,
> We shall overcome someday.

The Negro church enjoyed almost uninterrupted growth from its earliest beginnings down to the present day. Today many of the Negro's churches in the cities are imposing edifices, but a great many also are simply converted homes or the familiar store-front churches of Negro neighborhoods. One of the common observations of religious writers has been that, considering the Negro's economic inability to support all of the churches properly, he is probably "overchurched." As of 1963, there were 55,000 Negro churches in America, or one for every 200 Negro churchgoers. By comparison, there were 260,000 white churches, or one for every 400 white churchgoers. In general, Negro church denominations fall into the groupings of American Protestantism. The largest number of Negroes today— some 65 per cent—are Baptists, while 22 per cent are members of the several Methodist branches of the Negro church. There are, in addition, a fair number of Episcopalians, Lutherans, Presbyterians and Congregationalists. And, contrary to the patterns of the past, in recent years there has been a growing number of Roman Catholic Negroes (703,000 in 1962).

The affinity of the Negro for religion was clearly shown in the *Newsweek* poll, where an overwhelming 96 per cent of all Negroes professed a faith. Many of them (49 per cent) also said they attend church regularly—at least once a week or oftener. One little-noticed reason that has been advanced for the Negro's devotion to the church—other than his need for it—is that Negro society tends to be a matriarchal society, and women traditionally are not only more religious-minded themselves but often nudge their male charges into attending church. The matriarchal character of Negro society is largely a product of broken homes. The 1960 census showed that of all Negro women over fourteen years of age who have ever been married, one out of three no longer lives with her husband (the comparable white figure is one out of five). And of all Negro families lacking one parent, 85 per cent are headed by women.

But from the standpoint of the present revolution, the Negro's religious bent is far less important than the *intensity* of his devotion to Christian ideals. Long dependent on the word of God because he had nothing else, the Negro is today utterly convinced that his cause is just because it is just before God, and that he must ultimately win because that is God's word and will. In a literal sense, his revolution is thus a holy war.

Throughout all of the survey, the Negroes bore testimony to this. Whether the question asked them concerned demonstrations or the outcome of the revolution, many Negroes fell back on their religious faith in answering. "God will find a way for whoever is right," said a 40-year-old domestic in Dallas, Texas. The very strength of the Negro's religion caused a housewife in

Atlanta, Georgia, to prophesy, "The Negroes trust and believe in Jesus more than white people do, therefore we will win," while the Rev. Willie Henderson Gaddy of Lumberton, North Carolina, cited the Biblical injunction "the top shall go to the bottom and the bottom come to the top." In the simplest possible terms, a 79-year-old woman pensioner in Valdosta, Georgia, said, "God is with us." Many Negroes also mentioned the protection of God as the reason why they thought they could win without violence, while some cited the Bible as their authority for wanting to go slow in the civil-rights struggle. "What God says will come to pass; we can't hurry," said Mrs. Carrie Allen of Union Spring, Alabama.

Very nearly half of the Negroes (47 per cent) also told the poll that the ministers of their own churches were doing much to help in the fight. A 63-year-old waiter in Augusta, Georgia, spoke for a lot of Negroes when he said, "My minister is a great race fighter." Not always did this mean overt action, of course. It was readily apparent from the poll that for many Negroes, who may not fully understand the import of the revolution, their minister is mainly a source of advice and counsel. For instance, Mrs. Edna Mae Murchison of Philadelphia said, "He's a good preacher man. He gives us a lot of wisdom. He tells us to get ready because our day will come." A Detroit teacher observed of her minister, "He is teaching people to search their consciences to find good in all people," while Mrs. Sarah Jeffers of Chicago just said, "He is like a teacher."

Among those Negroes (34 per cent) who felt their ministers were doing little or nothing at all for the civil-rights cause, some attributed this to complacency or timidity and others to insufficient education. This kind of criticism occasionally came from ministers themselves. For example, the Rev. Robert L. T. Smith of Jackson, Mississippi, commented, "The vast majority of Negro pastors are not educated; also many are afraid to speak out because of intimidation and harassment."

A curious result of the poll was the amount of personal criticism directed by Negroes at their pastors. One man in the leadership sample, a politician, complained that his minister kept trying to tell him how to run his political affairs. "He should stick to religion," the politician growled. Again, a prominent civil-rights fighter who is himself a minister told the poll, "My minister is an egotistical fellow who is interested only in himself."

Some of these criticisms of the Negro clergy by their own followers undoubtedly are valid. The Negro ministry began, perforce, as a largely uneducated class and for many years it attracted great numbers of Negroes because it was one of the few opportunities open to them. Heavy emphasis was put on a man's "call" to preach rather than on any formal training. Even at the present time, only a small percentage of Negro ministers in America have seminary training.* Furthermore, the preaching of Negro clergymen has traditionally dwelt more on the green pastures and the golden streets of Heaven than on class struggle. Yet by the very nature of its founding, the Negro church has been a symbol of protest against the Negro's plight. In the slave era some Negroes could hold church services only if they hid from whites in basements and other places of concealment. Churches were also used to hide runaway slaves; in Charleston, South Carolina, the fugitives were hidden under the floor boards of the Negro church, and the Negro women covered the cracks with their long skirts when the dreaded "paddyrollers"—slave patrols—came stomping in. Whatever the shortcomings of the clergy, many Negro pastors became what W. E. B. DuBois called a "most unique personality" in the Negro society—"a leader, politician, orator, boss, intriguer and idealist."

Today it can hardly be questioned that, especially in the South, the Negro church has done as much as or more than any other segment of Negro society for the Negro's cause. The church has been the Negro's sanctuary, his tactical headquarters and a crucial means of communication between Negro leaders

* Today the Negro church, like the white, suffers from a lack of recruits to the clergy, with many educated young Negroes seeking their fortunes in the professions. Benjamin E. Mays, president of Atlanta's Morehouse College and an authority on the Negro church, has estimated that in 1963 there were no more than 200 Negroes in seminary training in all of the United States.

and the masses. It has also provided many of the most active and militant leaders of the revolt, headed by the Rev. Martin Luther King, Jr. Indeed, it can be argued, as some Negro ministers *have* argued, that, given the amorphous, formless quality of the Negro revolution, there was no place for an organized leadership to come from except the church. Wyatt Tee Walker, the slim, bespectacled young Negro Baptist minister who is King's aide-de-camp in the Southern Christian Leadership Conference, has said:

"In both the Negro and white community, the Negro church has often been made a joke, but the fact is that it's the most organized thing in the Negro's life. Whatever you want to do in the Negro community, whether it's selling Easter Seals or organizing a nonviolent campaign, you've got to do it through the Negro church, or it doesn't get done.

"The church today is central to the movement. If a Negro's going to have a meeting, where's he going to have it? Mostly he doesn't have a Masonic lodge, and he's not going to get the public schools. And the church is the primary means of communication, far ahead of the second best, which is the Negro barbershop and beauty parlor.

"There's no way to tell what would have happened to the Negro if he had not had the church. I'll say flatly that if there had been no Negro church, there would have been no civil rights movement today."

Dr. King himself made an additional point when interviewed by *Newsweek*: "The Negro minister is the freest man in the Negro community—not like schoolteachers, because his salary is paid by Negroes."

Pressing the church ever onward is a new breed of Negro preacher that bears no resemblance at all to the Father Divines and Sweet Daddy Graces of a few years ago. In their public preachments they may still invoke the power and glory of God, but they have translated Christianity into a hardheaded —if nonviolent—fight in the streets for equal rights. The Rev. Ralph David Abernathy has said, "The older generation of Negroes had a religion that was more concerned with the up yonder. They talked about walking down those golden streets.

We would rather walk on a few more black-top asphalt roads in some Negro neighborhoods down here." And Dr. King himself has observed: "The social gospel is as important as the gospel of personal salvation. Any religion that professes to be concerned about the souls of men and ignores social and economic conditions that cripple the soul is a spiritually moribund and dead religion, and it is only waiting for the day to be buried."

In leaving the pulpit to practice social gospel, Dr. King and his spiritual kin have often endured hardship and risked great personal danger. Many have been jailed, some have been man-handled by mobs and white police, and some have seen their homes and churches bombed. Just one incident is sufficient to demonstrate that the cloth has often been no guarantee of safety for the wearer, especially in the South. It occurred in the fall of 1963 when two Negro ministers in Anniston, Ala-bama—the Rev. Lemrod Reynolds and the Rev. William Mc-Lain—sought to enter the segregated public library on a Sunday afternoon. About ten whites set upon them and knocked them down with their fists. When the ministers fled to their car they were pelted with stones and bottles, and, when they were in-side, the whites jumped on their vehicle and smashed its windows with a chain. Only when the clergymen leaped into another car driven by a Negro were they able to escape. Even a minister with the stature of Martin Luther King has not escaped. Up to mid-1963, King had been jailed thirteen times, his home had been bombed and riddled with bullets, and he had been stabbed in the chest (in 1958, by a demented Negro woman in Harlem).

Like others of the new breed, Martin Luther King is an educated man. Born into a Baptist ministerial family in At-lanta, he was ready for college at the age of 15 and was gradu-ated from Morehouse College at 19. He trained for the ministry at Crozier Theological Seminary in Chester, Pennsylvania, and received his Ph.D. degree from Boston University. Unlike the green-pastures Negro preacher of old, he has read Niebuhr and Tillich, Nietzsche and Sartre and, above all, Gandhi.

King has written that his reading of the existential philoso-

phers convinced him that their view of man's existence as
filled with anxiety and threatened with meaninglessness had
great import for the Negro. But it was when he delved into the
Gandhian concept of passive resistance that he first saw how
it could be wedded to the Christian doctrine of love to provide
"one of the most potent weapons available to oppressed people
in their struggle for freedom."

King's spectacular use of this weapon has not been without
criticism. There are those who have asked if his passive resistance is really so passive and if he has not, in fact, precipi-
tated crises such as the one at Birmingham in the spring of
1963. King himself has answered that "passive resistance . . .
is passive in the sense that we are never violently aggressive.
But it is dynamically active in the sense that we are willing
to present our very lives for this truth. Keep in mind that there
is a great difference between nonresistance and nonviolence.
With that in mind, what we are doing is active resistance to
evil." Others on King's staff have said that the movement demands crisis as the most favorable climate for bargaining with
the whites. However interpreted, there can be no doubt that
passive resistance has done much for the Negro; more, it has
filled him with a zeal that has made his revolution wholly
unique. As one of King's aides put it: "A tone of morality
pervades the whole Negro struggle, and it emanates from the
church."

Above and beyond the demonstrations he has led, King has
been the most effective leader in rallying the masses of the
Negroes to their own cause. His powers of persuasion from
the pulpit and the platform are great. His Southern Christian
Leadership Conference, formed to coordinate the civil-rights
efforts of the clergy in the South, now embraces civic groups as
well. Its funds are substantial, a primary source being the
collection plate passed around when King speaks at Negro
churches all over the country on what have been designated
as "Freedom Sundays." His brand of old-time religion mixed
with quotations from Shakespeare and the existentialist philoso-
phers sometimes leaves the older Negroes in the congregation

wagging their heads. But they are always moved, and as the Rev. Edward J. Odom, national church secretary of the NAACP, has said, "King packs them in."

Prominent civil-rights fighters from the Negro clergy were among those interviewed in the poll. These men are, for the most part, the strongest believers in nonviolence. A Philadelphia minister spoke for many when he said, "I think any resort to violence will defeat our purposes. After the fighting is over we have to live with the white man and we don't want his blood on our hands." Others rejected violence as immoral and against the Christian spirit. This does not mean, however, that the nonviolent ministers lack militancy or unshakable devotion to the cause. The Rev. James L. Bevel, who is a rising young field secretary of the SCLC, said this: "I'm a believer in nonviolence and I wouldn't fight to protect my own daughter—that is, I wouldn't fight violently but in my own nonviolent way. [But] I think America is in a war now, and I am fighting desperately to help save it." Bevel was in the forefront of the Birmingham demonstrations of 1963, and at one point, when the mood on both sides was ugly, he stepped boldly into the center of the smoldering situation to quiet his own people.

Perhaps the most militant pronouncement of the whole integration struggle has been made by the Rev. E. W. Jarrett, a leader of the Negroes who demonstrated and endured police clubbings at Gadsden, Alabama, in June 1963. Said Jarrett: "We are going to keep on attacking the evil monster of segregation. As long as we got a foot, we gonna kick it. As long as we got a head, we gonna butt it. As long as we got a fist, we gonna hit it. And when we are old and toothless, we are gonna gum the hell out of it."

Militancy is to be found among civil-rights ministers other than those already named. The Rev. Fred Shuttlesworth has been a veteran fighter; as head of the Alabama Christian Movement for Human Rights he was a co-leader with King of the Birmingham marches of 1963. The Rev. James M. Lawson, Jr., a vigorous young SCLC leader, took part in the Freedom Rides and directed sit-ins at Nashville, Tennessee, in 1960 (and was expelled from Vanderbilt University for his efforts). The Chicago director of CORE, the Rev. B. Elton Cox, led the pickets protesting *de facto* school segregation in that city in the summer 1963. And that same summer in Brooklyn, New York, a group of ministers led a wave of demonstrations at construction sites where some of the participants went so far as to chain themselves together.

While the active militants of the Negro clergy have captured most of the nation's attention, others have been working in a quieter way, behind the scenes. In a large part of the South, for example, the churches have functioned as centers for voting-registration drives. The survey showed that the clergy—particularly in the South—puts heavy stress on voting rights as a major goal of the revolution.

In Philadelphia a local minister, the Rev. Leon Sullivan, spearheaded a little-publicized but highly successful use of the boycott to win more jobs for Negroes. Banding together some 450 ministers in the Philadelphia area, Sullivan used the technique of going to one industry at a time and asking for a specified number of jobs for Negroes. If the company refused, the Negro ministers spread the word to their flocks to boycott that company's products. Only a few did refuse, none permanently, *The New York Times* reported in August 1963, and the movement was credited with opening up several thousand new jobs for Negroes. The technique has been copied in Atlanta, Georgia, where a group of ministers—not connected with any civil-rights organizations—joined forces to get Negroes jobs in the city's six largest bakeries. Using the threat of boycott, they succeeded in desegregating employment at all six establishments in 1963, and then turned their attention to other companies and products.

The role of the clergy within the NAACP is a story in itself. The NAACP reported that in 1963 fully one-fifth of the presidents of its 941 branches across the country were ministers. In fact, the NAACP has used the Negro church as a primary means of attracting members; and Roy Wilkins, the NAACP's executive director, has confessed that without the help of the church in the South, his organization would not have been able to move in there. Many of the NAACP's minister-members have been active in some of those less spectacular, behind-the-scenes undertakings. In Virginia, for example, the Rev. L. Francis Griffin, head of the state NAACP organization, was a key conferee in the 1963 agreement to provide schooling for Negro children in Prince Edward County, where the public schools had been closed since 1959 to avoid integration. For Griffin, the agreement was the fruit of years of unremitting struggle in the educational area.

But not all the Negro clergy have been concretely involved —a fact sometimes deplored by the more active ministers. Wyatt Walker of the SCLC has estimated that no more than 10 per cent of the Negro clergy have been active for civil rights, and he has said that, in the Birmingham marches of May 1963, only about 20 of the city's 250 Negro ministers participated. Throughout the Negro demonstrations in the South it has been common in many communities for a sort of schism to appear in the Negro church, with some ministers leaping to take part and others—often the older pastors—sitting on the sidelines. Not that they have opposed the activists or tried to thwart them; more often they have simply done nothing. But Walker has said that at Birmingham a few older ministers were outright obstructionists—"men who have been brainwashed all their lives—they're Negro segregationists." On the other hand, it is a question whether the support of the entire Negro church is really needed. Even Walker has conceded, "The movement is in orbit now. The apathetics could help, but their continued apathy won't hurt."

The truth is that ministers like Martin Luther King and his followers are impatient men, convinced that social gospel is more compelling today than religious gospel. But it is also true that others have had misgivings about how far the church can go without losing sight of what they consider to be basic Christian principles. The Rev. Joseph H. Jackson, head of the National Baptist Convention, which with its 5 million members, 25,000 ministers and 27,000 churches is the largest Negro church organization in the world, has been criticized in Negro circles for advocating a go-slow policy on civil rights. Jackson's thesis, as outlined to *Newsweek,* was that "there is a danger that we may become so anxious to win an immediate victory for the race that we make secondary the winning of spiritual victory for the nation and for the advancement of the Kingdom of God among the children of men. The Negro church must at any cost add the salt of love and good will to the struggle for better human relations so that we may contend without being contentious and struggle for the right without becoming selfish or bitter."

However, a militant emphasis on immediate needs seems to be the dominant trend. Reverend Jackson's home church in Chicago, the Olivet Baptist Church, was picketed by Negroes during the summer of 1963. Later, when Jackson's National Baptist Convention held its annual meeting at Cleveland in September, the convention formally set up a new Civil Rights Commission to take a more active part in the revolt. What this appeared to be, more than anything else, was an attempt by the established church order to catch up with and ride herd on the new breed of militant ministers. As Jackson told *Newsweek*, the National Baptist Convention was interested not only in taking a more active part in the civil-rights struggle, "but in helping to plan its strategy, its program, and helping to determine its spirit."

Some authorities have suggested that the Negro church is also facing another kind of conflict: since it is a segregated institution, it may be working for its own demise by pursuing integration. (Much the same sort of question has been raised about the Negro press, which exists today almost solely as an institution serving Negroes.) The Negro clergy generally rejects this proposition, the survey found, or at least finds it too far distant to worry about. "I think the church will be one of the last things to go," said the Rev. Dr. Harry V. Richardson, president of the Interdenominational Theological Center in Atlanta. "This is because it is so much of a social gathering ground—a cultural and social group. While we may see more and more desegregation, I don't think you can see any predictable end of the Negro church." Reverend Jackson explained his belief in the church's survival as follows: "In the event of total integration, that which is peculiar to the Negro church will continue; it will not be destroyed or lost. [The Negro] has vision to see when his surroundings are dark. He has learned to trust on the very brink of despair. He has learned to bear crosses without retreating and without becoming the victim of doubt. These qualities will enrich the integrated church. . . ."

For the militant ministers like King, Abernathy, Shuttlesworth or Bevel, however, the survival of the Negro church tomorrow is less of a concern than the Negro's struggle today. In the mid-1960s, the Negro church had come a long way from the day when Richard Allen and his followers were yanked from their knees in Philadelphia. But much the same spirit of revolt that moved Richard Allen moves the Negro church now. In the view of its most outspoken leaders, the Negro church has not lost its Christianity; rather, it has adapted Christianity to serve the Negro's most pressing earthly needs.

CHAPTER 7

THE NEW
LEADERSHIP

*Some of us are hands and some of us are feet, but
we are all essential. And of course we also need a
head.* —A Mississippi preacher.

HISTORIANS HAVE ALWAYS argued about leader-
ship and always will: Do the times create the man, or does
the man create the times? In the case of the Negro revolution,
the answer seems to be that both forces are at work. Without the current group of Negro leaders, there might well be no
revolt as we know it today—and without the groundswell of
revolt, there would be no such leaders.

One of the millions of followers addressed himself to the
first point. James Mitchell, 25, of Philadelphia said, "Negro
people have become more active because they have found
the right leaders, men that are really interested and want to

111

help." And one of the strongest leaders—Whitney Young, Jr., of the National Urban League—addressed himself to the second point, saying that if the leaders didn't watch out, they'd be caught in the position of saying, "Hurry up, there go our followers!"

Whatever the cause, the fact is that a whole new leadership has emerged. Negroes who were unknown a decade ago now command the authority and respect of thousands. In this development, Southern Negroes have played a pivotal role. They have become an inspiration to the rest.

For many years, Southern Negroes were looked on by Negroes themselves as the least ambitious and the most passive, the least alert and the most difficult to arouse. Now the situation has changed dramatically. The survey found that a majority of the leadership group as well as a majority of the rank and file in the North feel that Southern Negroes are more militant today than their Northern counterparts. Mrs. Ruth M. Batson of Roxbury, Massachusetts, expressed the general feeling about those in the South: "They have nothing to lose and everything to gain. We in the North are still more cautious." In Los Angeles, entertainer Sammy Davis, Jr., was just as blunt: "Southern Negroes have shown bravery and should shame the Northern Negro." Atlanta leader T. M. Alexander, Sr., said, "In my opinion, the average Northern Negro is disillusioned because discrimination is more subtle in the North than in the South; therefore, he is more complacent. The Southern Negro knows that he is not free and he is not fooling himself but doing something about it." Comedian Dick Gregory was unequivocal: "The Southern Negro is the only individual in the U.S. today—bar none—who has one goal, one purpose: this is to achieve freedom." Among the rank and file, a 31-year-old machinist from the Bronx, New York, affirmed: "Southern Negroes seem to have more spunk and backbone." And Albert Ross Winters, 71, of Detroit expressed his criticism of Northerners vividly: "Negroes in the South has to fight for what he wants. Negroes in the North has laid down and wants people to bring his breakfast to his bed."

In the entire survey, one had to look hard for any sign of

the traditional Northern attitude toward Southern Negroes. Henry G. Johnson, 49, unemployed, of San Diego, California, was one who didn't seem aware of developments when he said, "The Southern Negro is more of an Uncle Tom and will call you a nigger in front of a white man." And a 78-year-old woman in Providence, Rhode Island, said rather snobbishly, "Those Southern Negroes around here are very uncouth and noisy."

But this was the exception, not the majority view. A 33-year-old crane operator from Saginaw, Michigan, said it for many: "They are acting different, because they are tired of running north to find the better things of life. They want to have these things in their own native land."

Up to about 1960 it was the North rather than the South that produced the leaders of the Negro cause. It used to be that Northern Negro leaders, often from the NAACP, would make forays into the South as a kind of uncharted battleground where bridgeheads of freedom might be won by legal battles. In the political field, during this period, one might have listed long-time Representatives William Dawson of Chicago and the mercurial Adam Clayton Powell of New York as the outstanding elected Negroes in this country. Both were politicians who played inside machine politics with old-line white Democratic politicos. Dawson was more "regular" than Powell, who had bolted to support Eisenhower. But both were certainly well known as ever ready, willing and able to make a deal. Both acquired considerable personal, financial and political affluence.

In addition to the lawyers and politicians, there were Negroes in other fields who had risen to prominence—men such as Ralph Bunche at the United Nations; Jackie Robinson, who broke the color line in baseball; and John Johnson, who built the first successful Negro publishing empire. Negro organizations were also at work; under Walter White, the NAACP—heavily populated by middle-income professionals—had forged an alliance with Northern white liberals and built a financial and legal defense base of solid proportions. The National Urban League, less militant than the NAACP, was developed largely with white funds and concentrated mainly on helping Negroes find jobs. A. Philip Randolph had given the Negroes a powerful and dignified voice in the councils of labor as head of the Brotherhood of Sleeping Car Porters. He had also fought battles, not always successfully, against union discrimination in the AFL-CIO.

Such was the state of Negro leadership before the big explosion in the South.

New leaders were to emerge from two chief sources: the Negro churches and colleges of the South. The students demonstrated both high militancy and a degree of creativeness and daring that had not been seen before. The Congress of Racial Equality (CORE) began the Freedom Rides and took the leadership in many sit-ins. Operating all over the nation, CORE has tended toward "one-shot" demonstrations as symbolic rallying points for follow-through by local organizations. In Atlanta, the Student Nonviolent Coordinating Committee (SNCC) has sent young people deep into the Black Belt to develop on-the-spot Negro leadership for the long haul, particularly through voter registration. Working and living closely with local Negroes, SNCC staff members in rural areas often wear a plain blue shirt and sharecropper's overalls. CORE and SNCC have cooperated in many instances. Their leaders and members share a common readiness to undergo physical suffering, beatings and even death rather than yield an inch in the struggle.

The most dynamic, impressive and, in some ways, most controversial leadership to emerge has been that of the Rev. Martin Luther King, Jr., and his Southern Christian Leadership Conference. King rocketed to world renown when he organized the first bus boycotts. He organized the SCLC both to strengthen the role of the Southern Negro church in the struggle and to use it as a base for his wide-ranging activities.

The King formula has been essentially a kind of massive saturation barrage. He strikes rapidly with support from all quarters of the Negro community. Birmingham is an example of the King approach. Suddenly within the space of a relatively few hours, Negroes were mobilized to picket, boycott, pray, demonstrate and register to vote in an all-out, full-scale war on discrimination.

The criticism of King by other Negro leaders is twofold. First, some say he tends to hit and run—as at Albany, Georgia, in 1962. A Negro leader has said, "We're always watching to see when his moment of compromise will be, when he will throw the people a bone and take off." Second, some Negroes say that he exploits his dramatic demonstrations to raise money for his Southern Christian Leadership Conference, that he drains local funds for the SCLC, that he does not account for money received and spent as carefully as he should, and that King's organization is top-heavy with self-perpetuating administrators. Though the Birmingham venture cost it plenty, SCLC sometimes seems to spend most of its funds raising more funds." *

These criticisms of the Rev. Martin Luther King, Jr., of course, reveal that the leadership of the Negro revolution is far from united. At best there is an uneasy truce between the young militants, such as CORE and SNCC; the older, well-financed organizations, such as the NAACP and the National Urban League; King's SCLC and others in the movement. Unity is often hard to come by.† For example, at the time of the march on Washington, SNCC chairman John Lewis wanted to talk about "the time . . . when we will . . . march through the South . . . the way Sherman did. We will pursue our own 'scorched earth' policy and burn Jim Crow to the ground—nonviolently." Catholic Archbishop Patrick O'Boyle, who was scheduled to deliver the invocation for the gathering at the steps of the Lincoln Memorial, said he would withdraw unless Lewis tempered his remarks. Various members of the March committee, which was headed by A. Philip Randolph and Bayard Rustin, pressed Lewis to omit the Sherman reference and other phrases in his script for the sake of unity. Lewis agreed.

* The SCLC budget rose from $180,000 in 1960 to nearly $900,000 in 1963.

† It should be noted that in addition to conflict among the various organizations, there is also considerable cooperation; several coordinating committees have been formed, some for temporary or local projects and others on a long-range basis. Examples are the Conference of Federated Organizations (COFO) and the Council for United Civil Rights Leadership.

The lines of division are not as clear as some at the top of the movement would make out. Nor are they simply a matter of one organization being more or less militant than another. For example, at the 1963 national convention of the supposedly conservative NAACP, militancy was so rampant that delegates booed Reverend Joseph Jackson off the speaker's stand because of his go-slow position.

Amidst this welter of conflict at the top, where does the rank-and-file Negro stand? The results of the poll did much to put the whole struggle for Negro leadership into clearer perspective. As a first step, Negroes were asked—without any prompting or aided recall—to name which person or organization had been most outstanding in the fight for Negro rights. The results:

WHO HAS DONE MOST FOR NEGRO RIGHTS

	Total Rank and File %	Non-South %	South %	Leaders %
NAACP	45	46	44	57
Martin Luther King, Jr.	26	27	25	27
President Kennedy	9	7	11	1
U.S. Supreme Court	5	5	5	10
Medgar Evers	2	2	2	—
CORE	1	1	2	3
Robert Kennedy	1	—	2	—
The Kennedys	1	1	1	—
Urban League	1	2	1	3
Roosevelt	1	1	1	2
Black Muslims	1	1	1	1
Thurgood Marshall	1	1	—	4
Democrats	1	1	—	—
Adam Clayton Powell	1	2	1	1
SNCC	—	—	—	3
Not sure	4	3	5	—

Here, of course, the NAACP nearly laps the rest of the field, both among the rank and file and the leadership group. It is noteworthy that mixed in with the Negro groups and individuals cited are more than a few white people and institutions. The

Negro leadership as such came into much clearer focus when Negroes were asked to rate each of six groups positively or negatively:

NEGROES ASSESS NEGRO ORGANIZATIONS

	Total Rank and File %	Non-South %	South %	Leaders %
NAACP				
Positive	91	93	89	91
Negative	3	4	2	7
Not sure	6	3	9	2
CORE				
Positive	59	61	57	78
Negative	8	7	8	17
Not sure	33	32	35	5
SCLC				
Positive	56	65	49	83
Negative	11	8	12	10
Not sure	33	27	39	7
National Urban League				
Positive	54	64	47	77
Negative	10	13	8	19
Not sure	36	23	45	4
SNCC				
Positive	19	23	18	74
Negative	4	3	4	11
Not sure	77	74	78	15
Black Muslims				
Positive	10	13	8	15
Negative	43	52	35	74
Not sure	47	35	57	11

Negro confidence in their own organizations ranges from high to low. The NAACP inspires the support of better than nine out of every ten Negroes in America, whether they are slum dwellers in the North, sharecroppers in the South, or belong to the rarefied strata of the leadership itself. As Miss Gloria Burns, 22, clerk-typist from Washington, D.C., said, "The NAACP is for the people and by the people." The NAACP is *the* Negro mass organization in both the North and the South. Negroes recognize that it has borne almost the entire brunt of the legal battle for Negro gains in the courts. Furthermore, when challenged for leadership by the newer and more militant groups, the NAACP took off its coat, turned down the street of militancy and continued to march at the head of the movement. Negroes are also aware that NAACP executive secretary Roy Wilkins has gone to jail, as have most of the other top leaders of the Negro revolution, and that the organization paid dearly in the struggle with the murder of its Jackson, Mississippi, organizer, Medgar Evers.

Even among the leadership group itself, the NAACP is accorded the top position. The leaders also give high support to CORE, SNCC, King's SCLC and the National Urban League. These organizations are far less well known among the rank and file; knowledge of SNCC in particular is largely confined to the leadership segments of the Negro community. However, where known they are uniformly well supported. The criticism of CORE and SNCC tends to be that they act "irresponsibly," while the National Urban League is taken to task by a minority for not being as forceful as it should be.

Negroes may differ in their views of most organizations, but toward one there is massive negative feeling: the Black Muslim movement—led by Elijah Muhammad and his top lieutenant, Malcolm X *—which believes in Allah, in separation and in the superiority of Negroes over whites. It should be noted that almost half of the rank-and-file Negroes apparently don't know what the Muslims are. ("You mean those Catholic ladies?" said an unemployed Chicagoan when asked his opinion of the Muslims.) But most of those who think they do are strongly against them, while the better-informed leadership is overwhelmingly so. State Senator Basil W. Brown in Highland Park, Michigan, was adamant: "You can't advocate racial superiority without advocating racial inferiority," he said. "I don't think there's much difference between the Muslims and what Hitler tried to do—at least in terms of philosophy." Mrs. W. F. Jeltz of Oklahoma City, Oklahoma, commented, "I do not like the

---

* In early December, 1963, Malcolm X was suspended as a spokesman for the Muslims because of his mocking comments on the assassination of President Kennedy.

theory of black supremacy—it's just as wrong as white supremacy. I don't like their spirit of violence and disrespect of law and government. Hate will never solve anything and they appear to be a hate organization." In Chicago, a 47-year-old man on state relief also had an aversion to the overtones of violence which he considered implicit in the Muslim movement. "I go along with Mr. King," he said. "You have to be friendly. Bloodshed is just no good." And Mrs. Erma M. Anders, 53, of Los Angeles added, "I don't believe in them or their idea that Jesus was black." In Philadelphia, a 36-year-old woman was more personal—if a bit inaccurate—about it: "I just don't like them with all that fuzz around their faces."

Some leaders were more tolerant of the Muslims. Writer Louis Lomax had this to say: "I am impressed with the way they give Negroes a sense of race pride and a desire to achieve despite the hardships. I believe, in time, when they are more sophisticated, they will soften their notion on race to the point where they will agree with me that not all white people are devils, just most of them." Among the rank and file, some defended the Muslims on the grounds of their high standards of personal and family morality and their successful efforts to combat juvenile delinquency.

When the poll put before the Negroes a proposition similar to that of the Muslims—that the Negroes form their own separate state in the South or in Africa—the idea met with better than 21 to 1 rejection, as the following table indicates:

ON A SEPARATE STATE FOR NEGROES

	Total Rank and File %	Non-South %	South %	Leaders %
Oppose separate state	87	91	84	99
Favor separate state	4	4	3	1
Not sure	9	5	13	–

Not only did Negroes oppose the separatist idea, but they greeted the suggestion with ridicule. The wife of a logger in a Woodville, Mississippi, sawmill put it this way: "That's a silly

idea. The one who said that should be made to live by himself."
And Fred G. Banks, a juvenile probation officer in Phoenix,
Arizona, had this logical extension of the plan: "Carry this
to the nth degree and you'll send all ethnic groups to their
original countries. That would leave the U.S. to the Indians."
In New York City, a 45-year-old mechanic went further: "If
everybody went back to where they came from, there wouldn't
be nobody left in America." A truck driver in Arp, Texas,
couldn't see it at all and put his objections simply: "I ain't
never come from Africa in the first place." The wife of a long-
shoreman in Oakland, California, saw it as a form of jail: "I
don't like to be put away."

The bulk of Negroes objected to the separatist idea for one
overriding reason. A teacher in Chicago put it for many: "We
don't have any business with such a state. We are inseparably
entwined with the whites in America." A 63-year-old mechanic
in Louisville, Kentucky, added, "We all came here together
and we should stay here together, because we go to war for our
country together."

Rejection of separatism, like other findings of the survey,
proved that Negroes want to achieve equality within the frame-
work of American society. They made it clear that they were
going to accept neither radical panaceas nor any leaders who
might suggest them. On the other hand, if the leaders should
lose their militancy or settle for less than full integration, the
poll makes clear that there would quickly be a new set of Negro
leaders.

In addition to the six organizations evaluated in the poll,
Negroes were also asked about 14 well-known Negroes:

NEGROES ASSESS 14 INDIVIDUAL LEADERS

	Total Rank and File %	Non-South %	South %	Leaders %
Martin Luther King, Jr.				
Positive	88	93	86	95
Negative	4	3	4	4
Not sure	8	4	10	1

NEGROES ASSESS 14 INDIVIDUAL LEADERS (*Cont'd*)

	Total Rank and File %	Non-South %	South %	Leaders %
Jackie Robinson				
Positive	80	85	76	82
Negative	8	9	7	14
Not sure	12	6	17	4
James Meredith				
Positive	79	84	75	81
Negative	6	6	6	18
Not sure	15	10	19	1
Medgar Evers				
Positive	78	81	76	92
Negative	3	3	2	2
Not sure	19	16	22	6
Roy Wilkins				
Positive	69	71	67	92
Negative	7	10	4	8
Not sure	24	19	29	—
Thurgood Marshall				
Positive	65	67	64	95
Negative	5	7	3	2
Not sure	30	26	33	3
Ralph Bunche				
Positive	62	62	63	76
Negative	10	14	6	17
Not sure	28	24	31	7
Dick Gregory				
Positive	62	73	52	82
Negative	8	10	7	14
Not sure	30	17	41	4
Harry Belafonte				
Positive	54	64	47	77
Negative	10	13	8	19
Not sure	36	23	45	4
Lena Horne				
Positive	55	53	56	68
Negative	18	24	13	25
Not sure	27	23	31	7
Adam Clayton Powell				
Positive	51	53	50	52
Negative	23	28	18	44
Not sure	26	19	32	4
Floyd Patterson				
Positive	53	53	54	50
Negative	20	26	15	32
Not sure	27	21	31	18

NEGROES ASSESS 14 INDIVIDUAL LEADERS (Cont'd)

	Total Rank and File %	Non-South %	South %	Leaders %
James Baldwin				
Positive	42	46	39	69
Negative	8	10	8	21
Not sure	50	44	53	10
Elijah Muhammad				
Positive	15	20	11	17
Negative	35	48	26	74
Not sure	50	32	63	9

Approval ratings range from high to low. As the table shows, a few of these names were known to almost all Negroes (as in the case of Dr. King), while others were unknown to 50 per cent or more (as in the cases of writer James Baldwin and Elijah Muhammad, head of the Muslims). Of all those on the list, Muhammad is the only one rejected outright—by better than a 2 to 1 count among those familiar with him. This, of course, parallels the negative attitude toward the Muslims as a movement.

The show-business, sports and cultural figures in the Negro community are by and large respected, but, with the sole exception of Jackie Robinson, they do not rank with the professional leaders of the Negro revolution. Support from such people as Lena Horne, Dick Gregory, Harry Belafonte, Floyd Patterson and James Baldwin is certainly welcomed by Negroes —and there is undoubted pride in their accomplishments within their own fields. But results confirm a fact that artists and entertainers have learned many times before: popularity as a show-business figure does not guaranteee any transference of effectiveness in public affairs.

There is a similar pattern in the cases of both Thurgood Marshall, former head of the legal arm of the NAACP * and now a Federal judge on the U.S. Court of Appeals, and Ralph

* That legal branch became a separate organization, the NAACP Legal Aid and Defense Fund, Inc.

Bunche, an Under Secretary of the United Nations. Both rank quite high in the opinion of the leaders, while roughly three out of every ten of the rank and file simply do not know who they are. They must be classified, according to the poll results, as inspirational figures to the leadership group but more as elder statesmen to the rank and file.

Representative Adam Clayton Powell, the chairman of the House Education and Labor Committee and a political power in his own native Harlem, receives approval by 51 per cent of the rank and file and 52 per cent of the leadership, but also evokes the highest degree of negative comment, after Elijah Muhammad. Powell is clearly controversial. A piano mover in New York City put it for many others in the Negro community when he said of Powell, "When things get thick, he thins out." While the poll did not ask about Chicago's William Dawson directly, some negative comment was volunteered about him. Mrs. Oliver Crawford of Chicago, for one, said about Dawson, "His silence is staggering." Quite evidently, both Powell and Dawson are in danger of becoming casualties of the Negro revolution. The implication is that the revolution has stepped up the level of leadership requirements and that politics as usual or leadership as usual will not suffice or survive. What the new elected Negro officials will be like, if these implications become reality, will be fascinating to observe.

Medgar Evers, the slain NAACP leader from Mississippi, and James Meredith, the first Negro to be graduated from the University of Mississippi, both represent another type of leadership in the Negro community today. They are the special heroes of the cause, singled out for their particular valor. As with any war or revolution, they are likely to go down in the annals as fabled martyrs to the cause.

Roy Wilkins, head of the NAACP, is not nearly so well known nor so well regarded by the rank and file as is his organization. In a way, this is not entirely surprising, for the strength of the NAACP is precisely that it has endured many years of existence and has a broad base, encompassing many important figures in the Negro leadership community. The

Wilkins case is not in any way degrading to the man, as witness the high respect his fellow leaders hold for him. The NAACP simply is not a one-man organization.

Diametrically opposite is the case of the most revered individual among Negroes today, Martin Luther King, Jr. King is much better known and much more respected as an individual than is his organization, the Southern Christian Leadership Conference. H. Julian Bond, an officer of SNCC, was critical of Dr. King for precisely this reason. "He has sold them on the concept that one man will come to your town and save you. That just will not work."

For most Negroes, Dr. King's contribution outweighs such considerations. Leader Reverend Walter Fauntroy of Washington, D.C., spoke this way: "There is no doubt that his emergence has speeded the course of the Negro's struggle in this country." New York City's 11th Assembly District Leader Lloyd Dickens put King's role in the parlance of his own Harlem politics: "He's overcome the stiffest obstacles, why he's beaten the odds." More typical was a San Diego, California, teacher, Donald E. Rickman: "He is showing outstanding leadership ability, and this is what the Negro has long needed."

There is no doubt that Dr. King comes closer to being the single mass leader of the Negro revolution than any other man today. What about the leaders of tomorrow? The likelihood is that they will be young; this is already the trend. Furthermore, just as white America has drawn many of its present-day political leaders from the battlefields of World War II, so may the Negro increasingly find his leaders among the veterans of Montgomery, Birmingham, Oxford and a score of other, less-publicized battlefields. The times will continue to produce the men, as these men are creating the times.

CHAPTER **8**

WHAT NEGROES THINK OF WHITES

WHITE PEOPLE MAY have thought little about Negroes until recently, but most Negroes cannot ignore the white man. The white man holds the key to the freedom, comforts and pleasures they aspire to, Negroes feel, and it is also the white man who has prevented them from achieving these things. How the Negro views whites is important since white society must eventually come to grips with Negro demands. Mutual understanding has become indispensable.

125

It was no surprise to find Negroes far from convinced that most white people really want them to get a better break. Here is what happened when Negroes were asked how they thought most whites really feel:

NEGROES ASSESS INTENTIONS OF MOST WHITES

	Total Rank-and File %	Non-South %	South %	Leaders %
Most Whites Want:				
Better break for Negroes	25	28	23	52
To keep Negroes down	42	35	47	9
Don't care one way or other	17	21	13	31
Not sure	16	16	17	8

Nearly six out of every ten Negroes feel that whites either want to keep them down or couldn't care less what happens to them. A housemaid from West Palm Beach, Florida, for instance, said this: "Whites want to keep us down. They don't want to see the colored man get ahead. When you put on decent clothes, they ask you what you are going to preach. This makes me mad."

When asked what motivated whites, Negroes gave a variety of answers. A railroad trackman from Louisville, Kentucky, said the real clue to whites must be "that they are afraid they will lose their maids." A 57-year-old woman in Oakland, California, was more general: "They don't like us, they are afraid of us." Blunt words came from a window cleaner in Riviera Beach, Florida, who said, "Well, I think the main reason whites hold us down is they think all Negro men want to marry white women. That is a dirty-thinking person." A 30-year-old postal clerk in Brooklyn, New York, had another theory: "The low man in a barrel has to have someone to feel better than. The white man can feel better than a Negro." A 33-year-old housewife in Washington, D.C., also felt the white man has a psychological need for discriminating: "Without the Negro, the white man has no one to look down on. He certainly can't look down on the Jew. The Jew has made an ass of him."

Others write off white discrimination toward them as a manifestation of blind emotionalism. A 44-year-old worker in Minneapolis said with obvious bitterness, "They are just ignorant and hate Negroes so much they don't want us to become equal to them. They think more of their dogs than they do Negroes." Some believe whites suffer from such a guilty conscience that they cannot face up to what other whites will say if they treat Negroes decently. As Mrs. Janet Rancifer, 25, of Chicago said, "Most whites have to go along with the more ignorant whites. They don't want to be called 'nigger lover.'" A woman teacher in Houston, Texas, also attributed white attitudes to lack of contact: "Most of them know so little about us —have been exposed to only a certain class. I'd like to see the races acquire a better understanding of each other. You can't legislative love. As I heard it said once, 'I hope we haven't started hating whites by the time they've started loving Negroes.'"

The leadership group has a far more sanguine view of whites than the rank and file. One reason for this is undoubtedly that Negro leaders have had more opportunities accorded them as individuals than the rank and file. They have also had far more contact with whites, especially those friendly to their cause.

When the poll probed deeper to find out if Negroes distinguished between Northern and Southern whites, only 38 per cent of the rank and file and 49 per cent of the leadership group made such a distinction and thought that Northern whites held better views about Negro rights. Significantly, Northern Negroes felt most strongly that Northern whites were not much different from white men in the South. This feeling was later borne out by the poll of whites, as reported in Chapter 9.

A minority of nearly four in ten held out for the view that the Northern white is indeed better in his attitude toward Negroes. A Memphis teacher put it succinctly: "Whites in the North like for Negroes to be independent, but those in the South like you dependent." And a 23-year-old truck driver from Houston said, "The whites in the North have been living with and working with Negroes and having more social contact with them and they realize Negroes don't pollute their system." A sizable group felt that it wasn't so much that white men were different in the North but rather that their laws were less repressive. As the wife of a janitor in Detroit said, "It is the laws on the books what makes the white man in the North treat the Negro better, not that he likes him any better." Still others judged by experience or at least by the experience of others, such as a 50-year-old man of Wichita, Kansas, who said, "In the North, most Negroes have jobs and homes, but in the South they want them to plow."

The prevailing view, however, remained dour and skeptical of the Northern white. Typical was the comment of Harold B. Fontes, a 31-year-old stevedore in Providence, Rhode Island: "The Southerner lets you know where you stand. The Northerner stabs you in the back." Another sharp comment came from Washington, D.C.: "I don't really think there is much difference. I think the white man in the North makes a better hypocrite." And a young Bronx, New York, housewife returned to the familiar theme: "Whites in the North are just more sneaky in their bigotry than those in the South." In a different tone, the Rev. Leonard Chapman of New York City did not distinguish between Northern whites and people in general: "Man is basically selfish and is not concerned about what type of break someone else is getting as long as it does not affect him. The average American is not overwhelmingly concerned about the Chinese boy who goes to bed hungry or the Indian child whose fingers are cut off to make him a more effective beggar."

If the majority of Negroes express doubts and reservations about Northern whites, they are almost equally suspicious of whites who are opposed to the KKK, for example, but who also want change to be more gradual than drastic. When asked whether these "moderates" were "more helpful" or "more harmful" to the cause of Negro rights, opinion split down the middle: *

* The question was phrased in these relative terms so as to allow the respondent a degree of latitude and reasonableness in replying.

NEGROES VIEW WHITE MODERATES

	Total Rank and File %	Leaders %
Moderates more helpful to Negro rights	29	46
Moderates more harmful	31	40
Not sure	40	14

Defenders of the white moderates tended to be practical about it, such as a 50-year-old woman on relief, who said, "A half a loaf is better than no loaf, as I see it." Dr. James Nabrit, Jr., added, "Anybody who has any moderate voice is more helpful, especially when compared to Bull Connor." Eugene Robinson, 68, of Washington, D.C., saw a constructive role for moderates: "I feel they serve the same purpose as a halter on a race horse, which, if not controlled, can defeat itself. Some of the diehard Dixiecrats who won't yield to pressure by the colored people would otherwise listen to the moderates of their own race."

But a majority of better than seven out of every ten Negroes has yet to be convinced that the success of their revolution depends on linking hands with white moderates. Negro leader Joseph Faison of Philadelphia said bluntly, "Being a moderate is a nice way for a guy to hide." In Chicago, the owner of an auto repair shop added, "Moderate is just a fancy name for do nothing." New York leader Gladys Harrington went even further when she said, "There is nothing more detrimental than liberal whites and moderate Negroes."

U.S. Attorney Cecil F. Poole of San Francisco was convinced the Negro revolution had passed the white moderate by: "They have formed a buffer between their group and the unknown. By this time, the world has gone around them. The philosophy of a few years ago is outdated." During the Washington march Roy Wilkins, head of the NAACP, jibed at Southern congressmen who say they want to vote for the Administration's civil-rights bill but make the usual excuses for why they cannot. "And we say to those people, just give us a little time and one of these days we'll emancipate *you*."

Negro reluctance to depend on white moderates points up a widespread conviction that the struggle will be won by their own direct action. This does not mean rejection of support from whites, nor a lack of recognition that the white man in the end must grant freedom and be willing to integrate. It does mean that as far as initiative for change goes, Negroes are counting on their own. For, they reason, without a big self-push, they might have to wait another hundred years—good will, good wishes and decency notwithstanding.

Despite the bitterness and the skepticism about the good intentions of whites, a majority of all Negroes believe that white attitudes today are better than they were five years ago. Here is the result of a direct question put to Negroes on white attitudes:

WHITE ATTITUDES NOW VERSUS FIVE YEARS AGO

	Total Rank and File %	Non-South %	South %	Leaders %
Better attitude	52	51	53	89
Worse attitude	2	2	3	3
Not much change	32	32	33	7
Not sure	14	15	11	2

One of the big reasons for improvement in white attitudes, Negroes say, is that whites are coming to understand what Negroes want. As a housewife in Raleigh, North Carolina, put it, "Many whites know that what we are fighting for is ours by birth and whatever they do will not stop the Negro from fighting for what is his. Therefore, white attitudes have changed for the better."

Negroes find significant the smallest changes in white attitudes. For instance, a 78-year-old woman residing in Washington, D.C., said, "Do you remember that at one time the white man would not use a capital 'N' when he wrote the word 'Negro'? It's changing now." Or as Jack Thatcher, 35, an electronics technician of Mt. Vernon, New York, put it, "They no longer think of the Negro as a clown with a zoot suit and knives."

And Mrs. Clyde Durham, 41, of St. Louis had this to say: "They only know us as servants and like that. We're just beginning to get on a level where they can know us as people." Mrs. Gladys E. Roberts, a Phoenix, Arizona, teacher, also reported, "More and more white people are beginning to meet Negroes and to realize that Negroes are not really the ape-type, subhuman being as some whites had been led to believe."

Perhaps more than anyone else in the entire survey, a 41-year-old housewife in Houston, Texas, showed clearly just how sensitively and minutely Negroes are attuned to change. She said, "I don't hear them say 'nigger' as much. My husband says that they have one cup and two kegs of water at work, and nobody thinks anything about it." A mark of progress to Negroes is to have white and Negro workers share a drinking cup at work, for such an act spells out more graphically than countless words that progress indeed is being registered.

In noting white attitudes, Negroes distinguish between different groups. They were asked in the survey to rate 15 major institutions and groups in white society according to whether each had been *more* helpful or *more* harmful in the struggle for Negro rights.

Easily the largest amount of Negro confidence in white society today resides in the power of government. Here is how five different parts of government fared:

NEGROES ASSESS THE GOVERNMENT

	Total Rank and File %	Leaders %
Kennedy Administration		
More helpful	88	95
More harmful	2	4
Not sure	10	1
U.S. Supreme Court		
More helpful	85	94
More harmful	2	2
Not sure	13	4

NEGROES ASSESS THE GOVERNMENT (*Cont'd*)

	Total Rank and File %	Leaders %
Congress		
More helpful	54	31
More harmful	9	40
Not sure	37	29
State Government		
More helpful	35	34
More harmful	32	39
Not sure	33	27
Local Authorities		
More helpful	30	38
More harmful	35	45
Not sure	35	17

It is immediately apparent that Negroes rely heavily on the Federal government, far less on state and local authority. If they have to choose between Federal and local authority, they will trust the former, particularly in the South, where both state and local government meet with disfavor. Politically, of course, this casts Negroes as natural enemies of states' rights. It is also likely to add impetus to local political organization by Negroes.

Again, they placed high confidence in the Kennedy Administration (as well as the Supreme Court). The administration was rated high on a relative basis—within the context of what some call "the white power structure." In other respects, the Negro depends primarily on his own people.

Congress came off well among the rank and file, but negatively with the leaders. It is abundantly clear that the skepticism of the leadership group has not been effectively communicated to the mass of Negroes. The rank and file tended to identify Congress as part of a sympathetic Federal government. And while they are not nearly so sure of the legislative branch, it will take some rather shocking disappointments to disillusion them.

Negroes were also asked to assess the role played in the revolution by certain non-Negro religious and ethnic groups.

Here is how Negroes evaluated Catholic priests, white churches and two minority groups, Jews and Puerto Ricans: *

NEGROES ASSESS RELIGIOUS AND ETHNIC GROUPS

	Total Rank and File %	Leaders %
Catholic Priests		
More helpful	58	74
More harmful	5	9
Not sure	37	17
Jews		
More helpful	44	73
More harmful	9	8
Not sure	47	19
White Churches		
More helpful	24	36
More harmful	24	41
Not sure	52	23
Puerto Ricans		
More helpful	10	20
More harmful	15	11
Not sure	75	69

On a selective basis, Negroes look to help for their cause from two key religious minorities, Catholics and Jews. Both, of course, have officially espoused civil rights. Both have been targets of the Ku Klux Klan and other groups which have led the fight against Negro claims to equality. The rank and file of Negroes are aware of the stands taken by Catholics and Jews, and the leadership overwhelmingly acknowledges this support. Negro recognition of Jewish support puts to rest the rather widespread claims that anti-Semitism is rife in Negro society.

By contrast, white churches as a general category receive at best a split decision from Negroes. And the pattern does not

* The categories of Catholic priests and white churches were decided upon when pre-testing for the survey showed that Catholicism was more meaningful to Negroes in terms of individual priests with whom they had come into contact, while "the Catholic Church" sounded monolithic and unfamiliar to them. On the other hand, "white churches" was generally understood to mean white Protestant religious establishments.

vary greatly by leadership or rank and file, nor by region or group (as the complete results show). There is a lingering suspicion in the Negro community that organized white religion has been slow and even laggard in recognizing discrimination as a moral issue.

Most Negroes have no firm views about Puerto Ricans. But, as a further breakdown by area shows, those who are thrown together with them in many of the Eastern and Midwestern big-city ghettos have little enthusiasm for this group. Almost one-fifth of the Northern Negroes felt that the Puerto Ricans had been "more harmful."

Negroes are ambivalent about labor unions. On the one hand, they recognize support for their cause from unions such as the United Auto Workers, whose president, Walter Reuther, was a major speaker in the ceremonies at the Lincoln Memorial in the march on Washington. On the other hand, Negroes see unions as another inbuilt white man's device to wall them off from an opportunity to join the mainstream of white society. Largely unorganized and essentially bypassed in organizing drives because they fall in the category of the less skilled, Negroes today do not especially look to unions and labor organizations as a primary means of salvation. Some of the strongest protests in the North have been registered against the lily-white membership restrictions in the building-trades unions.

On balance, however, more Negroes see unions helping rather than hurting their cause. This is especially the case among the leadership group:

NEGROES ASSESS ROLE OF LABOR UNIONS

	Total Rank and File %	Leaders %
More helpful	40	54
More harmful	26	28
Not sure	34	18

While Negroes may have mixed feelings about unions, they are sharply critical of discrimination in white businesses and public accommodations. Many of the economic roots of the Negro revolution became apparent in the following table:

NEGROES ASSESS WHITE MANAGEMENT IN BUSINESS AND PUBLIC ACCOMMODATIONS

	Total Rank and File %	Leaders %
Bus Companies		
More helpful	39	14
More harmful	22	48
Not sure	39	38
Movie Theaters		
More helpful	20	16
More harmful	38	49
Not sure	42	35
General Businesses		
More helpful	19	14
More harmful	39	62
Not sure	42	24
Hotels and Motels		
More helpful	16	19
More harmful	43	47
Not sure	41	34
Real-Estate Companies		
More helpful	16	4
More harmful	48	87
Not sure	36	9

The rank and file of Negroes and especially the leaders clearly feel that white companies in general and real-estate and service businesses in particular have been major stumbling blocks in their struggle for equality. It is no happenstance that the picketing, demonstrations and sit-ins have been systematically directed against places of business that have discriminated against Negroes in employment and in service. As a caretaker from Lumberton, North Carolina, put it for many others in the poll, "I'd like to see white people look pleasant at us and not look so mad when we go to buy something."

Taken in the aggregate, out of the whole roster of 15 non-Negro institutions or groups which Negroes were asked to evaluate, only seven come off as being more helpful than harmful in the fight for Negro rights. It is plain that the Negro community, from top to bottom, feels that organized white society has loaded the dice against them.

One would expect in such circumstances to find Negroes ready to cancel all hope of acceptance by white society. But when Negroes were asked what they thought would happen to white attitudes in the next five years, the overwhelming majority expressed the highest kind of optimism, as the following table dramatically indicates:

WHITE ATTITUDES FIVE YEARS FROM NOW

	Total Rank and File %	Leaders %
Better attitude	73	93
Worse attitude	2	—
Stay same	11	4
Not sure	14	3

A certain number of Negroes were not so sure about a change in white attitudes. They found it difficult to predict just how viable whites would be in the face of Negro demands. Even Malcolm X of the Black Muslims—who usually had clear-cut answers to every question—registered a "not sure" opinion on this score and explained: "It's too hard to follow the erratic thinking of a white man. He changes with the wind and the water." Among those who thought that the situation would stay the same, a certain bitterness emerged. A young woman living on welfare in Washington, D.C., said: "What they really feel on the inside never changes. Eventually they will wind up calling you a nigger."

But a substantial majority held hope for improvement. Their expectation is rooted in the related beliefs that the revolution cannot be stopped and that whites will realize Negroes are not too different from the rest of the human race. In Baton Rouge, Louisiana, a 32-year-old maid expressed the Negro's confidence: "They'll get better because they know now that we mean business." This faith in their success led many Negroes to foresee a change in white attitudes. Mrs. Lillian W. Crowder of Memphis held that "whites will become more open-minded as they see the Negro as a person, not a thing. They will also learn that Negroes want citizenship rights, not white wives." A young New York City truckdriver said simply, "As you know people better you begin to understand. There will be greater understanding. Time is an important factor and the time is ripe for understanding." Others referred to growing white awareness of Negroes through the public media—magazine, newspaper and book coverage of the Negro revolution. Such exposure, they felt, would prove an important stimulus to a change in the white man's spirit. Perhaps a deeper reason, some thought, would be the sheer necessity for a new attitude if the United States were to survive. Mrs. Thelma Wright, a health educator in Savannah, Georgia, summed up this feeling: "Negroes and whites founded our country together, they fought for our country's freedom together. They need one another now as never before."

CHAPTER 9

WHAT WHITES THINK OF NEGROES

Eventually we will be healing a sore that has been open one hundred years. —A 68-year-old white woman in Virginia City, Nevada.

THE NEGRO'S ATTITUDE toward the white man is fundamentally simple: it is based on the desire for equality. But when the white man in America looks at the Negro he is torn by a conflict between his emotions and his intellect. His intellect tells him that the Negro has indeed suffered years of discrimination, directly contradicting the American creed of equality for all. But his emotions make him feel uneasy at the prospect of such equality for the Negro.

138

Newsweek conducted a special survey of whites to determine the extent of the gulf between the two races and the likelihood of bridging it. This poll confirmed many of the suspicions of Negroes about the negative feelings of whites—perhaps beyond even what many Negroes imagine.

In the course of interviews lasting over two hours each, some more than three, whites were asked how they felt about contact with Negroes and why. This question released a stream of un-inhibited feeling about Negroes as people. The violent emotion-alism of many comments was striking. A retired clerk from Inverness, Florida, declared, "They stink. In cafeterias here you go around and collect your food. Then niggers paw over your food and then you have to give them a tip to carry your tray. Big old dirty black paws pawing your food, then you've got to eat it." A 57-year-old hospital employee in Mobile, Alabama, said, "I couldn't stomach it if I thought I was eating after or beside a diseased Negro—which 90 per cent of them are. All this will lead to is social mixing. Their own kind don't keep a clean place."

The outpour was by no means limited to whites of the Deep South. Mrs. Ethel Shuey, 62, of Palmyra, Pennsylvania, com-mented, "Their skin looks greasy and unclean." A 68-year-old woman in Rodney, Ohio, raised the specter of intermarriage, a white cry that was to be heard many times over: "Well, there's too much marrying colored. They are old, dirty things." Another elderly woman in Arkansas City, Kansas, pronounced, "You can smell them a mile away. They're just not our people." A 54-year-old housewife from Wyandotte, Michigan, qualified her feeling: "I don't mind them unless they are very dark or if they're very odorous." And a Washington, Pennsylvania, house-wife, expressed the frequently mentioned aversion to personal contact: "I don't like to have to touch them. It just makes me squeamish. I know I shouldn't be that way but it still bothers me." A 56-year-old maintenance man for the Detroit, Michi-gan, highway department told this story: "There was a good Negro living around here and my little boy shook hands with him and then he turned his hand over and looked at it and the

Negro said, 'It won't rub off on you.' I never forgot that. It's the idea of rubbing up against them. It won't rub off but it don't feel right, either."

The element of fear was evident in a number of responses. A woman in Baltimore, Maryland, again elderly, spelled out many of the details: "You don't know what they're going to do. You're leery. They carry razors, knives, rape women. You can't trust them. Don't know what they'll do. I'm scared of them." A young repairman in East Springfield, Massachusetts, said, "I feel as though I can't trust them. I think they'll start a fight. I might pick up some type of disease." A housewife from Cecil, Wisconsin, confessed, "I'm scared of them really." Silas Masters, 72, retired, of Palmetto, Florida, explained, "I don't like to use restrooms in those places where a darn nigger has been. It's venereal disease." A Baltimore housewife believed that "no matter how much you try to educate them or do for them, they still have the savage in them."

This wall of white emotion is the real enemy of the Negro revolution. The survey explored in detail the components of prejudice, both North and South. In addition, it sought to discover whether prejudice diminished with social contact.

A series of ten stereotypes about Negroes was set before the white people, who were then asked which statements they agreed with and which they rejected. The following table reports the results from the nationwide cross-section, from the South and from a special group of those who had had social contact with Negroes. This last group, 25 per cent of the total, proved throughout the survey to be the most sympathetic to the Negro and his cause.

WHITE STEREOTYPES ABOUT NEGROES

Agree with statement:	Nationwide %	South %	Previous Social Contact Group %
Negroes laugh a lot	68	81	79
Negroes tend to have less ambition	66	81	56
Negroes smell different	60	78	50
Negroes have looser morals	55	80	39
Negroes keep untidy homes	46	57	31

WHITE STEREOTYPES ABOUT NEGROES (*Cont'd*)

	Nationwide	South	Previous Social Contact Group
	%	%	
Negroes want to live off the handout	41	61	26
Negroes have less native intelligence	39	60	23
Negroes breed crime	35	46	21
Negroes are inferior to whites	31	51	15
Negroes care less for the family	31	49	22

While the white South accepts these stereotypes to a greater degree, it would be a vast error to conclude that the North is much different. Even those whites who have had social contact with Negroes share many of these feelings—some of them without even realizing it.

A 61-year-old resident of Alhambra, California, thought he was the epitome of tolerance: "They're human beings the same as the rest of us. Why should you feel uncomfortable with any-one not of the Caucasian race? I've even square danced with them." A rancher in Reno, Nevada, declared: "I have no racial prejudice. Took showers with star athletes—went to school with them." Another Californian in his sixties, this one from San Diego, told where he would draw the line: "If you mean sexual intercourse, no. Shaking hands is O.K. Kissing, no thanks. But shaking hands, O.K." Mrs. Edward Schneider, 50, of Miami, Florida, declared that she worked with Negroes and didn't feel uncomfortable, but added, "The crummy ones do stink. They don't have to at all. I know they can take pills to avoid the odor they carry as a race. The better educated ones take pills and do not have that odor."

If views such as these comprised the total white attitude toward Negroes, then the only logical conclusion to draw would be that America is on the threshold of a bloody race war. But whites hold a whole roster of other beliefs that are in direct conflict with their emotions about Negroes as people. One is that Negroes have rights as citizens which must be guaranteed under the laws of the United States. Whites were asked about some of the Negro's demands:

THE WHITE VIEW OF NEGRO RIGHTS

	Nationwide %	South %
Approve:		
Voting in elections	93	88
Unrestricted use of buses and trains	88	75
Job opportunities	88	80
Decent housing	82	76

The most startling figures in this table are those that reflect Southern attitudes. Even in the South, a large majority of whites feel Negroes should be guaranteed these rights. What is more, sizable majorities of whites feel that further legislation is needed from Congress to strengthen Negro rights. On this question, however, Southern whites disagree sharply with white people elsewhere:

WHITE SUPPORT FOR CIVIL-RIGHTS LEGISLATION

	Nationwide %	South %
Approve:		
Federal vote-enforcement law	57	31
Federal Fair Employment Practices law	62	40
Kennedy civil-rights bill	63	31
Public-accommodations bill	66	29

Comparison of these two tables reveals an interesting anomaly: 88 per cent of the white Southerners believe that Negroes have the right to vote, but only 31 per cent favor legislation backing up that right. There is a similar though less striking contrast on the subject of jobs. Legislation seems to be the sticking point; all whites are more ready to approve other forms of Federal intervention for equal rights. The table on page 143 shows how they stand on the role played by the government since 1954.

In the poll of whites, a deep and abiding sense of law and order came through powerfully. F. Arthur Cowen, 57, a commercial artist in Crestwood, Missouri, commented on the use of troops in Oxford: "It's a matter of upholding the law. It's a

WHITES ASSESS FEDERAL ACTION

	Nationwide %	South %
Approve:		
Eisenhower use of troops in Little Rock, Ark.	71	44
Kennedy use of troops at Oxford, Miss.	65	37
The original Supreme Court decision	64	35
Over-all role of Federal government in civil rights	64	35
Over-all role of Federal courts in civil rights	60	33

matter of principle." A laborer from Cromwell, Indiana, agreed: "That [sending troops to Little Rock] was the law. If one state gets by the law without obeying, why should I pay an income tax? Why should I obey the law? It's the same thing." To Arthur Jackson, 66, a real-estate broker in Breckenridge, Minnesota, the whole American system was on trial: "We can't do otherwise as a democracy. We have to practice what we preach to other nations." A Copley, Ohio, housewife saw government action as the only way out: "This situation has to be cleared up and if we can't do it through our government, how can we do it?" A Chicago laborer added, "If you leave it to the local government to start, it won't get done."

Over and over again, whites saw few alternatives under the American system other than to grant Negroes their rights. Alfred Blanckaert, 69, a retired St. Louisan, said, "Federal laws are over state laws and one state can't tell the other part of the United States what to do. The big plantation owners don't want integration because of cheap labor. The Negroes are getting smart and want their rights. I don't approve all the Negroes do but don't approve of all the whites do either." Mrs. Mary Alice Beezley, 32, a housewife from Princeton, Indiana, saw any other course indefensible: "I feel that the Negro, although he's black, still has the red blood in him. He's human and he has as much right to the same rights as we have." Loree Donahue, 36, a San Diego, California, housewife, thought that if grownups stayed calm, the children would settle it: "I think that all should abide by the Supreme Court rule. The Negro didn't ask for his skin color. When parents keep their noses out, kids get along O.K. Kids kiss and make up. So older people cause all the trouble."

As their own words indicate, white people in America are not overjoyed about the necessity to support their Federal government in its efforts to insure Negro rights in reality. In fact, the majority (51 per cent) criticized the Kennedy Administration for its handling of the issue. And yet only a minority of whites could bring themselves to oppose specifically the steps their government had taken.

How do whites rationalize this acceptance of equality under the law with the personal aversions to Negroes so many of them apparently feel? Timing plays a part. By better than a 2 to 1 margin, whites feel that Negroes are moving too fast in their revolution. As an East Springfield, Massachusetts, housewife said, "They want everything in too short a time. They did nothing for too long a time, then a sudden uprising. They could have been doing these things all along. They can't be handed something for nothing. They have to earn it." A 45-year-old housewife in Milwaukee, Wisconsin, summed up the feeling this way: "It couldn't possibly be stopped now. But I think their leaders have urged them on too fast. A lot of them aren't ready to get all these things at one time."

By a 64-36 per cent count, whites feel Negroes are asking for more than they can possibly absorb. Minta Shumate, 28, a housewife in Crestwood, Missouri, said it for the majority: "Until the Negro wants to better educate himself and qualify for it, things aren't going to change overnight, even if the freedoms are guaranteed them. They will have to work for them." The methods of the revolution are just as disturbing to whites as its tempo. While Negroes feel demonstrations have been vital and effective most whites feel that the demonstrations have hurt the Negro cause. "A lot of it is show-off," thought a retired man in Palmyra, Pennsylvania. "They want to be seen, make a lot of noise." A 65-year-old widow from Macon, Georgia, made a judgment about the demonstration in her town: "I think locally it has hurt. They look like they are wild people out of the jungle and this is the way all Negroes are inside." A 23-year-old woman, also of Macon, thought the demonstrations "showed the brutality of them. Our maid says the young Negro boys have killed several old Negro men in their neighborhood. They took clubs and beat them to death out of meanness and it didn't even get in the newspapers." Joseph Brognano, 45, a laborer from Wampum, Pennsylvania, put it this way: "They just showed how they want to overrun the whites and tell them what to do. The nerve they have to buck whites. Now we won't trust them."

When asked in detail about the methods of the Negro revolution, whites went on record as 2 to 1 in opposition to the lunch-counter sit-ins, 4 to 3 against Negro willingness to go to jail voluntarily for their cause, 5 to 3 against picketing of stores and over 10 to 1 against the "lie-downs" in front of trucks on construction sites. However, by slim margins, whites do accept the general idea of demonstrating and think that the Negroes are justified in having conducted the march on Washington.

Sam Stump, 56, a retired farmer from Cromwell, Indiana, was typical in his reaction: "The march on Washington helped. It was like a calm voice there, telling what they wanted." A 65-year-old retired man from Bell, California, thought Negroes should slow down some, but added, "The Washington demonstration was remarkable. I don't think that many white people could have put it over that good." In Crestline, Ohio, Mrs. Mary Ogle was also enthusiastic: "It was very well organized—to have that many people and no violence." A. Gerard Patterson, 34, from Appleton, Wisconsin, saw positive results from the demonstrations: "After all, it's the squeaking wheel that gets the oil."

These very demonstrations appear to have driven home the whole point of the Negro protest. But the majority view of whites was clearly that the Negroes were pressing too hard, asking for too much. Whites have remarkably clear understanding of Negro demands. The following table, drawn from volunteered comments, shows what whites think Negroes want:

WHAT WHITES THINK NEGROES WANT

	Whites Nationwide %
Equal treatment	41
Better jobs	14
Better education	11
Make America aware of their problem	8
Better housing	7
Dignity, respect, status	6
Publicity for the problem	6
Representation in government	5
Be able to go anywhere, do anything	2

There is a remarkable parallel between what whites think Negroes want and what Negroes themselves said they want.

Furthermore, there is widespread recognition among whites that Negroes are discriminated against. Fully 71 per cent of all whites in the country and even a majority of 56 per cent in the South acknowledged this fact. By better than 3 to 2, white people feel Negroes do not have job opportunities equal to whites. By a somewhat closer margin whites also believe Negro children receive an inferior education. And by almost 3 to 1, whites believe Negro housing is not nearly so good as that for whites.

Some whites recalled specific occasions when they had observed Negroes being discriminated against. Laurence Boyd, a laborer from Lake Zurich, Illinois, told this story: "We went to a restaurant with a colored guy who works with us and they wouldn't serve him. I thought this was a dirty, crying shame. Just cause he's black don't mean he ain't hungry. We all got up and left." A 49-year-old man from Dexter, Missouri, said, "They have been pushed down to lower-paying jobs and given the dirty jobs and I don't think that is right." William Reger, 25, a laborer from Cromwell, Indiana, gave his observation: "On TV you see it. Not getting served. No place to build where they want to. No chance to advance. They discriminate against Negroes in the services such as rank is concerned. I've only seen one colored officer in six years of service. This is all very wrong. Some are ten times smarter than whites but they have no chance."

In fact, when whites were asked how they thought it must feel to be discriminated against as a Negro, they bristled with indignation and even outrage at the thought of being treated like Negroes. "I think it would be hard on the morale," said Mrs. Donald Nei, 38, a housewife of Larwill, Indiana. "When we get some little minor snub, we are so upset. Imagine how it would be to live with discrimination all your life. It would take a mighty strong person to try to improve yourself." Mrs. Geraldine Gilbert, 45, of San Diego, California, put it this way: "It must be horrible. If it were me, there would be a terrible rage inside me. It would make me a mean, spiteful person and I'd be ready to do battle at any moment. I'd also treat anyone who suppressed me as dirt if I got the chance." In Detroit, Michigan, an office worker felt that "it would tend to make a person hate—which is serious." Cleveland Moffett, a 33-year-old New Yorker, was deeply indignant: "It makes a free-thinking person wince with rage to see the way Negroes are treated simply because they have dark skins." A 34-year-old housewife in Jonesboro, Tennessee, wasn't sure how it would feel to be a Negro discriminated against, but then had this afterthought: "I would feel like somebody without a country." Mrs. Ralph D. Sanders, 34, of Fayetteville, North Carolina, summed it all up for many mothers: "It must be horrible. From a mother's point of view, it must break their hearts to hear what the children are called and the way they are treated, and yet have to teach them that this is their way of life."

If whites are thus able to understand in human terms just what it means to be a Negro in America, how far are they willing to go toward integration? This is obviously a key question, and in large part American history of the next ten years will be written by the answer. The survey investigated the limits of white viability, from willingness to work side by side with a Negro to allowing a teen-age daughter to date a Negro boy:

WHITE FEELING ABOUT CONTACT WITH NEGROES

	Nationwide %	South %	Previous Social Contact Group %
Would object to:			
Working next to a Negro on the job	17	31	8
Sitting next to a Negro at a lunch counter	20	50	4
Sitting next to a Negro on a bus	20	47	5
Sitting next to a Negro in a movie theater	23	54	6
Own children going to school with Negroes	23	55	9
Using same restroom as Negroes	24	56	9
Trying on same suit or dress that Negro had tried on in clothing store	32	57	16
Having own child bring Negro friend home to supper	41	76	16
Having Negro family as next-door neighbors	51	74	26
Close friend or relative marrying a Negro	84	91	70
Own teen-age daughter dating a Negro	90	97	80

It is immediately apparent from these results that the vast majority of white America is prepared to accept a great deal more contact with Negroes than has taken place up to now. The degree of Southern viability may come as a surprise. Nationwide, in view of the revulsion expressed by many earlier in this chapter, the over-all results testify to white willingness —grudging though it may be—to accommodate. But white America is not at all ready for social integration to the extent of dating and intermarriage. Even among those who have had social contact with Negroes, 70 per cent would object to a close friend or relative marrying a Negro and 80 per cent would be worried if their teen-age daughter dated a Negro. Some whites rationalized segregation in this area as former President Harry S. Truman once did—all the way back to the Bible.

These results also indicate the likely areas of accommodation for the immediate future as well as the areas of sharp conflict.

Equal employment, which is also the number-one priority for Negroes, seems ripe for a breakthrough. Nearly nine out of

every ten whites—including eight out of every ten Southerners
—feel that Negroes have the right to equal jobs. What is more,
as another question in the poll revealed, a majority all over
the country do not fear that Negroes will take their jobs away.
Significantly, a solid majority (62 per cent) of whites favor
a Federal law enforcing an end to discrimination on the job.
However, white people are equally adamant that there should
not be a strict 10 per cent quota for Negroes in job hiring
(rejected by over 4 to 1) or that Negroes should actually be
given job preference over whites (turned down by a staggering
31 to 1 margin).

Part of the reason for whites' willingness to go along with
an end to job discrimination is the highly positive experience
of white people who have associated with Negroes on the job:

"You are there to get a job done, not to socialize. I don't
mind working with them"—Mrs. Ralph Riddle, Dexter, Missouri.

"I've worked with colored girls. They were really on the
ball, with good sense and efficient. Clean and neat, too"—a
housewife, Mahwah, New Jersey.

"They were wonderful to me. I worked as a teacher and
they were teachers. Because I was a substitute, I found them
much better and kinder than many white teachers"—a 46-year-
old woman in Alhambra, California.

"Color won't rub off. I work in the fire department, eat and
sleep with a Negro. O.K., I'd say"—Robert Howard, 30, of
Kokomo, Indiana.

"I used to sing and a Negro girl sang in my group. She was
so clean and nice, I think I lost my prejudices"—a housewife
in Tennessee.

"I have worked with them. I have worked with foreigners
that I have minded more up north"—a 64-year-old laborer from
Inverness, Florida.

"It is just like working with any other man. Heck, he's
entitled to work"—Arvin Beaubien, 48-year-old laborer from
Wyandotte, Michigan.

"He's just human. I've sewed for many of them, altering
dresses, and they have always been clean, polite. I've never

found any different odor about them either, though they do perspire a great deal"—a seamstress from Tacoma, Washington.

Education is another major area in which there appears to be a considerable amount of white willingness to go along with the Negro revolution, although the South registers a loud and determined "no" on this score. Better than seven out of ten whites would not mind their own children going to integrated schools, and an equal number reject the notion that the education of white children would suffer if both races go to school together. Finally, in reply to another question in the poll, fully three-quarters of all white people in America said they believed that school integration is inevitable. In fact, 57 per cent of the white South share this view.

The wife of a Rochester, New York, laborer explained her view on integrated education: "If my children started school with colored children they wouldn't even notice the difference. When they are young [color] does not matter to them." Mrs. Lenore Brucklacher, a minister's wife and mother of seven in Florence, South Dakota, said, "It is good for children to realize there are differences and yet we are all the same." A tobacco farmer's wife in Tennessee put it this way: "If they are good enough to go to school, they're good enough to go with my kids, I reckon." Another farmer's wife, in Larwill, Indiana, added, "There are some white children who could stand a little more training at home. The color of their skin isn't what makes them a decent companion for your children."

Whites may be receptive to the idea of integrated education, but they are not amenable to the next step, which is probably the only path to integrated schooling: whites and Negroes living in the same neighborhoods.

While 59 per cent of all whites in the country feel that integrated housing is on the way, 50 per cent say they would be upset if it happened where they live. However, those who now live in integrated neighborhoods report by better than 5 to 1 that they are not bothered by having Negroes live near them. This result should ease some of the fear that explosions are bound to occur in white neighborhoods now undergoing an influx of Negroes.

However, many whites who do not live near Negroes are highly doubtful that integrated housing will work. They think that when Negroes move in, whites move out. As a 73-year-old man in Detroit, Michigan, said, "If you get a block-buster,* most of the people get panicky and the homes are taken over entirely by Negroes." He went on to recall: "A brand-new school that was practically all white went practically all colored in twelve months in one area of the city." "Even if the whites did not move out," said State Senator James Slattery from Nevada, "the colored fellow would feel uncomfortable. Of course, the value of the property also goes 'way down." A widow in San Jose, California, harked back to what she thought of Negroes as people: "Negroes are their own worst enemy. [If they move in] the people that are for them will get disgusted and turn away." A housewife in Mobile, Alabama, agreed: "They are not capable of the general upkeep, maintenance and improvement of any home. This is why they are living in shacks."

To some whites, the idea of Negroes moving into their neighborhood evoked fighting words, such as those of a woman in Burnham, Texas: "It ain't gonna happen right here. Maybe the edge of town. Nobody ain't gonna sell 'em no lots so as they can build. I tell you, nigger settlement here just ain't gonna be like whites."

But if one half of the white people, North and South, would be upset by integrated housing, the other half say they would not. For example, a 68-year-old laborer in St. Louis said simply, "They have the right to go anywhere they want to go." And a 51-year-old housewife in Hillsboro, Oregon, added, "They have earned people's respect and those who can afford the better homes are the nicer class, too." Thomas M. Brown, a laborer from Clay, Kentucky, saw it happening this way: "By the time they move in, we'll all be used to them being in better jobs."

A majority sensed that integrated housing is sure to come.

* "A real-estate speculator who deliberately breaks a neighborhood color line by selling property to a Negro; this causes other white residents to move out, selling cheap, whereupon the block-buster buys up and sells at high profit."

Jerome Knuijt, 32, a science teacher in Lake Zurich, Illinois, said, "If this country is to exist, it's inevitable. And if one is intelligent, he doesn't fight the inevitable." Mr. Charles E. Drewett of Crestwood, Missouri, held the view, "There is an evolution we're going through. As Negroes get education, we will get educated with them. People are less biased than they were five, fifteen years ago."

In the bull's-eye areas of the revolution, jobs and education held out promise for steady progress. Housing, however, seems to be a sticking point. But is it really?

Some whites are sophisticated enough to perceive that for Negroes the right to integrate in housing is more important than the deed. Some of them also understand that there are Negroes who are reluctant to move into white neighborhoods. C. E. Matteson, retired, of Tucson, Arizona, said, "I do not feel that the Negro especially cares about living in white neighborhoods. But he doesn't want to be told he can't be-cause of his color." Mrs. Audrey Klaeser, 42, of Milwaukee, Wisconsin, added, "They like to stay with their people. They wouldn't like to move in white neighborhoods any more than whites would want to move in theirs."

Does the oft-expressed revulsion of whites to Negroes, and their apparent resistance to accommodation, mean that the Negro's social revolt will end in a bloody clash? To some extent the very history of the United States argues differently. Time and again the American people have adapted to changing times, changing customs—and changing neighbors. This has happened with successive waves of immigration by the Irish, the Poles, the Italians and others.

Of course, there are obvious differences in the situation of the Negroes—as was noted in Chapter 2—to argue against such optimism. Their color is different. A bitter war was fought in their name. They have been here far longer without achieving equality. And there are more of them to intensify conflict. But numbers can be a double-edged sword; for ulti-mate effectiveness in a democracy, numbers have counted in the past.

Furthermore, while some of the whites' emotions have vitiated their intellectual acceptance of equality for Negroes, other feelings are working in a different way. Many whites reported that their ministers were preaching that it is morally wrong to discriminate. According to the poll, whites feel by a 2 to 1 margin that the whole question of Negro rights is a moral issue. Mrs. Lucy J. Rittie, 84, of Cromwell, Indiana, said it thus: "Negroes are God's children and we want to do our best to accept them."

And Mrs. H. B. Kaszynski, 50, of Beaumont, Texas, added, "I don't know how you could be a Christian and feel better or superior to a colored person."

CHAPTER 10

BREAKING THE VICIOUS CIRCLE

I would like to see all the barricades torn down so a man could be as free as you'd be in a desert—walk any way you want to when you want to. —Earbie Bledsoe, St. Louis, Missouri.

NEGROES HAVE SHOWN time and again that they are prepared to demonstrate, picket, boycott or go to jail in order to achieve their goal of full citizenship. They have also made it clear that this goal includes partaking in the material abundance that typifies life in white America today. In one

154

particular they already enjoy this material wealth to a startling degree: more than 90 per cent of all Negro homes have television—a fact that has played an important role in motivating the revolution itself. Every day, television reminds the Negro of the whites' comfortable way of life—suburban houses with modern kitchens, shiny new cars and dishwashers, power mowers and neatly trimmed lawns. Most Negroes would like a greater measure of these things they see whites enjoying every day of their lives. They "want in." * And this goes to the core of the Negro dilemma.

To share in the wealth, quite obviously the Negroes need jobs that pay them an adequate living. To qualify for such jobs the Negroes need education. To get a good education they must live in neighborhoods where the schools are good. And to do that they have to have the money to pay for decent housing. This vicious circle has long existed and shows no real signs of being broken yet.

No one is more aware of this dilemma than the Negroes themselves—as witness the many-pronged drive of the revolution, its simultaneous demands for better jobs, education and housing. The poll revealed that these bread-and-butter essentials were considered indispensable to the general goal of equality. In the area of jobs, Negroes put it on the line. They want better jobs, and they want to be paid the same as whites for their work. The following table illustrates concretely just what Negroes want in their quest for employment opportunities. In one column is the distribution of job categories as Negroes reported their present employment to the poll. The second column shows where Negroes think they can go—with their present qualifications:

* A small but significant number of Negroes, particularly in the leadership group, feel differently and do not emphasize materialistic goals. They are apparently alienated from middle-class American society for deeper reasons than inability to share in the wealth. One leader expressed this feeling when he said in the survey that the Negro's biggest need was for "an honest facing up to the distorted values and negative aspects present in the majority society."

PRESENT NEGRO EMPLOYMENT AND JOBS NEGROES WANT

	Jobs Now Held %	Jobs Negroes Want and Feel Qualified For %
Unskilled labor	31	9
Personal service (domestics, etc.)	17	6
Unemployed	12	—
Skilled labor	10	29
White collar	10	14
Retired on pension	7	9
Professional	5	10
Business executive	4	18
Civil service	4	5

The two lists could not be more dramatically different. Today, employed Negroes are concentrated heavily in menial, unskilled jobs, such as sweepers, janitors, helpers, sharecroppers or as porters, maids and dishwashers in homes or in service trades. When those without any jobs at all, the unemployed, are added to those doing menial work, the number mounts to six out of every ten Negro breadwinners in the United States today.

By contrast, six out of ten Negroes feel they are qualified to hold down jobs as skilled laborers, professionals or business executives. This number swells to amost eight out of every ten when white-collar and civil-service job aspirations are added.

It is quite apparent that most Negroes mean to hoist themselves into the mainstream of middle-class America. And just as they want better pay for better jobs, they also want the good things that money can buy. The following table shows what Negroes would most like to have if they moved to a new place to live:

WHAT NEGROES WANT MOST IN NEW HOME

	Total Rank and File	Non-South	South
	%	%	%
Clothes dryer	26	27	25
Dishwasher	23	26	21
Clothes washer	19	19	19
Central heating	13	4	20
Telephone	12	9	14
Miscellaneous (bathtubs, running water, inside toilet, etc.)	29	13	53

NOTE: Items add to more than 100 per cent because some Negroes named more than one item they would want most in a new place to live.

Negroes do not want to take these things away from whites or to destroy the white society that has them. On the contrary, Negroes ask only for the chance to earn the better life with dignity.

To the Negro, one important dimension of dignity at work is integration on the job. By roughly 7 to 1, Negroes categorically stated their preference for working in a mixed job force. Even in the South, where such an experience has not been a common one, Negroes prefer integration on the job by a 4 to 1 margin:

NEGRO OPINION ON INTEGRATED JOBS

	Total Rank and File	Non-South	South
	%	%	%
Prefer mixed group— Negroes and whites	76	84	68
Prefer mostly Negroes	11	6	17
Not sure	13	10	15

Negroes feel no less strongly about integrated education; again the margin in favor is 7 to 1. The way Negroes see it, the key to better education for their children is not to improve their own segregated schools but rather to integrate. Answering another question, Negro mothers said—by a better than 3 to 2 margin—that they would be willing to have their children picked up and transported to another part of town just to achieve integration.

A solid majority of Negroes everywhere in the country—among the leadership group as well as the rank and file—believe that Negro children will actually do better work if they go to school with whites.

Negroes seem to be convinced that integration in itself would have a salutary effect on their own children. To be sure, Negroes also believe that in mixed schools the present inferior facilities, equipment, textbooks and buildings would be eliminated. But fundamentally Negroes believe that segregation has a damaging effect on the psychological outlook of their children that can be rectified only through integration. In fact, the U.S. Supreme Court made precisely this point in its historic 1954 decision: "To separate them [children in grade and high schools] from others of similar age and qualifications solely because of their race generates a feeling of inferiority as to their status in the community that may affect their hearts and minds in a way unlikely ever to be undone."

When it comes to housing, Negroes are somewhat less sure about integration. Though the vast majority favor it, they do so with some trepidation. Many shared the feeling of a tool inspector in Philadelphia: "I wouldn't feel comfortable living with white people. I'm more at ease with my own people."

The following table reveals how Negroes feel about living in mixed or all-Negro neighborhoods:

NEGRO OPINION ON INTEGRATED HOUSING

	Total Rank and File %	Non-South %	South %
Prefer neighborhood with whites and Negroes	64	75	55
Prefer all-Negro neighborhood	20	11	27
Not sure	16	14	18

Three important facts should be noted about these results on housing. First, while Negroes feel, by a 7 to 1 margin, that schools and employment should be integrated, the count drops to just over 3 to 1 for housing.

Second, even among the 64 per cent who say they want to integrate, nearly half add that it is not so much a matter of actually living next door to whites as having the right to do so. For example, Mrs. Eve B. de Lay, 49, a kindergarten teacher from New Orleans, put it this way: "I'm not eager to live among whites, but I feel that people should be able to live together in a neighborhood—if the whites don't move away."

The third important fact is that one-fifth of the Negroes prefer to live with their own. A 75-year-old woman in Cincinnati, Ohio, said, "I don't want to mix with white folks because they don't want to mix with me." A young textile worker from Sumter, South Carolina, added, in a switch that sounded like some whites talking about living in Negro neighborhoods: "I feel safer around Negroes." A house painter from Selma, North Carolina, saw only trouble between white and Negro children in a mixed neighborhood. "Because white young'uns are so mean and hard to get along with." A housewife from Pine Bluff, Arkansas, put it simply: "Because the old white devils pick at you so."

Ervin Abney, a Philadelphia construction worker, spoke for one Negro in every five when he said, "I'd get along better with my own kind. Some of them white people are hard to live around, if you know what I mean. Well, they'll act funny around you. They complain about things, take their kids away from yours, you know, things like that."

At the other end of the spectrum were Negroes who want to live in a white neighborhood because they do not particularly like living with people of their own race. A farmer in Black Creek, North Carolina, for example, said, "I figure some whites treat you better than your own color will." A 54-year-old Chicago housewife finds Negroes objectionable this way: "Some of our colored people are terrible. The way they live, their mouths, their actions. When living with whites, you keep to yourself. The colored want to be sociable and some of them are terrible." Mrs. Lucy Howell, 59, of Memphis, Tennessee, differentiated between Negroes and "niggers" and added, "I don't like niggers." An unemployed man in Westchester County, New York, wanted to escape the whole problem: "I'd just like a half acre with nobody on it but me."

But the group who want integration in housing to avoid association with undesirable fellow Negroes is microscopic compared with those who feel that, as a matter of principle, integration is preferable. A 34-year-old unemployed woman in Providence, Rhode Island, put her finger on the psychological trauma of the ghetto: "I feel it isn't healthy to live in an all-Negro area. In order to know people, it is necessary to mix." A number of Negroes made this point, emphasizing the importance of living in a mixed neighborhood *as a social experience*—particularly for their children. It was not merely a question of housing but of over-all personality development. A factory forelady in Philadelphia felt that associating with whites is part of growing up right: "I like my children to be able to associate with other types of children. I'd like for them to see how the other half lives." Mrs. Berlin Benson, a restaurant employee from Mt. Vernon, New York, underscored this feeling when she said, "I'd rather bring my children up in a white community. . . . They'd be able to cope with all situations. This way, being brought up only with Negroes, they don't learn how to cope with situations which might develop between Negroes and whites."

Other Negroes feel just as strongly that integrated housing is a necessity if whites are ultimately to accept them on equal terms. Mrs. Samuel Hill, a housewife in Wichita, Kansas, said, "I think I am intelligent enough to communicate with any of them. This is one of our largest problems." Another Mt. Vernon, New York, woman sees further lessons for whites in mixed housing: "It would make a better America. If they get to know us, they'd find out we don't all carry knives and are just as good as they. In fact, I know some I feel I am better than they are."

One Negro in every twenty reported having lived in mixed neighborhoods—and most of these liked the experience. An office cleaner in Cleveland, Ohio, reported, "The white neighbors that I have always known have always been very nice to my family." A Woodville, Mississippi, construction worker, added, "I live close to white families now and we get along

O.K." A 43-year-old butcher from St. Louis found his neighborhood turning black and regretted it: "I've found that it is pretty nice to live around mixed neighborhoods. When I first came here, it wasn't nothing but white and it was a nicer neighborhood."

The reason almost two out of every three Negroes prefer integrated housing is not the superior facilities of white neighborhoods. Rather, it is more the psychological effect of liberation from the ghetto and the deeply felt desire to prove to whites that Negroes aren't as bad as they think.

How soon and how fast will this liberation take place? The vicious circle argues against it happening soon. Indeed, Negroes themselves believe it may come slower than many whites now fear. When asked to give their estimate of just how much integration they expect to take place in the next five years, only a minority of Negroes thought it would be extensive:

NEGRO ESTIMATE OF INTEGRATION IN THE NEXT FIVE YEARS

	Total Rank and File %	South %	Non-South %
A lot of integration	33	34	34
Some, not a lot of integration	36	38	33
Only a little integration	17	18	17
Not sure	14	10	16

These results point clearly to the fact that Negroes do not expect the millennium overnight.

The next question, and a key one, is: just what does the word "integration" mean for them? Does it mean a massive outpouring of Negroes from their ghettos into white suburbs, schools, restaurants, social organizations and churches? The Negro's own answer is that this is not his primary or immediate goal. What he wants now is to be treated as a human being; and part and parcel of this is the *right* to integrate.

Negroes were specifically asked to choose which was more important to them—equal treatment or "a lot of mixing of the races." By a margin of better than 8 to 1 they chose equal treatment.

NEGRO DESIRE FOR LOT OF MIXING VS. JUST BEING TREATED AS HUMAN BEINGS

	Total Rank and File %	Non-South %	South %	Leaders %
Just being treated as human beings	86	87	86	68
Lot of mixing of races	10	10	10	25
Not sure	4	3	4	7

When probed to find out what they meant by their answers to this question, Negro replies were revealing. A journalist in Detroit said, "I don't feel that mixing of the races per se is what we're striving for. It's only equal opportunity we want." In Jackson, Mississippi, the Rev. S. Leon Whitney spoke the view of the majority: "I don't think Negroes want integration as much as they want desegregation. Negroes don't want favoritism, they just want justice." A tractor driver from Woodville, Mississippi, put it this way: "I am not thinking about mixing with anybody. I just don't want to be treated like an animal."

Here is a statistical summary of their volunteered remarks:

WHY NEGROES PREFER TREATMENT AS HUMAN BEINGS OR MUCH MIXING OF RACES

	Total Rank and File %	Non-South %	South %	Leaders %
Treatment As Human Beings				
Just want dignity, good treatment	27	26	28	16
Mixing not important, just treated normally	25	27	24	28
Want equal rights	13	11	15	8
Let me go where want to and do what want	3	2	3	2
Want to be treated as full citizen	3	4	3	1
Want equal opportunity for education	1	1	1	1
Fought in wars, should have benefits of country	1	*	1	–
Want more opportunities	1	1	2	1

WHY NEGROES PREFER TREATMENT AS HUMAN BEINGS OR MUCH MIXING OF RACES (*Cont'd*)

	Total Rank and File %	Non-South %	South %	Leaders
Lot of Mixing				
Should live in brotherhood—get to know each other	10	10	11	36
Not Sure	19	20	18	11

    * Less than 1 per cent.

NOTE: Percentages add to more than 100 per cent because some Negroes gave more than one reason for their preference.

The "mixing" aspect, of course, has the ultimate implication of intermarriage. This was faced and rejected by most Negroes. Typical was Carl Elbert, 51, who works for a lumber company in Arp, Texas: "They think we want their women. All we want our children to have is an education. We don't want for our children to grow up and marry the young'uns." A Mt. Vernon, New York, housewife went even further: "For me personally, I don't care if I never eat with one. And as far as courting and getting married which is what they are afraid of, I don't care to see that." The basic desire of the Negro is simply to find dignity in his relations with whites. Many put it in terms of personal experience, such as the Detroit housewife who said, "I never wanted to visit with white people or go to parties with them, but just work where we could make the good wages . . . maybe eat in a real nice place. That is all."

One Negro in ten among the rank and file disagrees, and believes that equal treatment cannot be achieved without massive integration. In the leadership, this proportion rises to over one-third. Militant Philadelphia leader Cecil Moore was one: "In order to be treated like a member of the human race, everything will have to be mixed. We want to keep up with the Joneses, too." Student James Sidney Hammond from Jackson, Mississippi, agreed: "As long as there is no mixing, the Negro will be treated as inferior."

While most Negroes neither expect nor especially want full integration with whites now, they do indeed mean "freedom *now*." Despite the considerably stepped-up tempo of the revolution in 1963, one Negro in every two told the survey that he felt progress on Negro rights was still too slow:

HOW NEGROES FEEL ABOUT PROGRESS
ON NEGRO RIGHTS

	Total Rank and File %	Non-South %	South %	Leaders %
Too slow	51	57	46	77
About right	31	32	32	20
Too fast	3	2	3	1
Not sure	15	9	19	2

"Why should it take so long?" asked Frances Rembert of Detroit, Michigan. "It doesn't take so long for our money to mix with their money in the cash register." "All Negroes are tired of waiting for the white man to get ready to give him something that is his," said Bettye Ann Wilson of West Palm Beach, Florida. And in New Orleans, Louisiana, A. M. Trudeau, Jr., made this graphic comment: "An NAACP official once said, 'If a man is choking me to death, I don't want him to release me gradually. I want him to turn me loose right away.' That's why integration is going too slow."

Negroes feel they are on the march—and they intend to go full speed ahead until, as many said, "Jim Crow is dead." The priorities of Negroes are also clear: Equal rights *now,* especially in jobs and education. Housing restrictions, they feel, should be lifted, although most Negroes expect that they will still live in dominantly Negro neighborhoods for some time to come.

Despite dissatisfaction with the progress to date, Negroes are nonetheless optimistic about what will happen within the next five years. When they were asked about six major areas of discrimination, a majority stated that they felt they would be better off five years from now in all but one area. The exception was voting rights; nearly half of the rank-and-file Negroes thought that things would be the same as now, and 81 per cent of the leaders agreed. However, a further breakdown revealed that most of those who expect no change were from the North and felt that they already had full voting rights. Otherwise, solid majorities believe that pay will be higher, jobs more abundant, better housing available, school integration more of a reality and white restaurants more accessible to Negroes.

To a large degree, of course, the realization of these high hopes rests with whites and just how viable they will be in the face of the revolution's demands. But Negroes all over America have tasted freedom and the self-respect that comes from speaking out for one's rights. Their determination will not lag, for it is made of solid stuff. They have arrived at the waking point and will not rest until they have overcome.

Susie Hazzard, a maid in suburban Cleveland, spoke for her people in a few words: "I want some of these flowers before I die—give me my flowers while I live."

THE
QUESTIONNAIRE

Here are the questions as actually asked in the survey of Negro people on which this book is based.

1a. Thinking ahead to five years from now, if you had to say right now, do you feel in (EACH ITEM BELOW) you will be better off, worse off or about the same as you are right now?

(FOR EACH) And why do you feel that way?

	Better Off	Worse Off	About Same	Not Sure
1. Your work situation	____	____	____	____
2. Your housing accommodations	____	____	____	____
3. Your pay	____	____	____	____
4. Being able to register and vote	____	____	____	____
5. Being able to eat in any restaurant	____	____	____	____
6. Being able to get your children educated with white children	____	____	____	____

167

b. As far as you personally are concerned, what do you feel are the two or three biggest problems facing Negro people that you feel something should be done about?

(FOR EACH PROBLEM) What do you think ought to be done about it?

(FOR EACH PROBLEM) Where is it most important to work on it—in Washington, here in the state, or right here in this town?

2a. Are you employed now?

Yes _____ (SKIP TO 2c)
No _____ (ASK b)

b. (IF NO) Who is usually the main wage-earner in this family?

IF EMPLOYED	IF NOT EMPLOYED ASK ABOUT MAIN WAGE-EARNER
c. What kind of job do you have now? What do you do?	c. What kind of job does _____ (Name of wage-earner) have? What does he (she) do?
d. What kind of job do you feel you are qualified for that you would like to get?	d. What kind of job is he (she) qualified for that he'd (she'd) like to get?
e. Is there a job you would like to get trained for? What's that?	e. Is there a job he (she) would like to get trained for? What's that?

3a. In what trades or fields do you think Negroes are getting a better break these days as far as jobs go? Any others?

b. What trades or fields do you feel are the worst as far as giving Negroes jobs? Any others?

c. Do you feel that if you do the same work as a white man, you will be paid the same as he will get for that work or will you probably get paid less?

Same pay _____
Less pay _____
Not sure _____

d. Would you rather work for a company run by a white man or by a Negro, or doesn't it make any difference to you?

White _____
Negro _____
No difference _____
Not sure _____

e. At work, would you rather work alongside mostly other Negroes, or would you rather work with a mixed group of whites and Negroes?

Mostly other Negroes _____
Mixed group _____
Not sure _____

4. In general, if you were to get a house cr apartment (flat) the same as a white person, do you feel you would pay more rent or the same as the white person would pay?

Same _____
More _____
Not sure _____

5. If you could move to any part of the country, where would you like to live most—in a city, a suburb or a smaller town in the North OR a city, or suburb, or a smaller town in the South?

North city _____
North suburb _____
North small town _____
South city _____
South suburb _____
South small town _____
Not sure _____

6. Would you like to live in a private house, a housing project, or an apartment (flat)?

Private house _____
Housing project _____
Apartment (flat) _____
Not sure _____

7a. Now I want to go down a list of things some people tell us they want where they live. (READ ONE BY ONE) Do you have (ITEM) in your present (house, apartment)? NOTE: Where obvious in better neighborhoods ask: Of course, you have ("Inside toilet"), etc.

b. (FOR ALL THE "DON'T HAVE NOW" IN 7a) Which one would you most like to have if you moved to a new place?

	Now Have	Don't Have	Most Like to Have
Inside toilet	_____	_____	_____
Electricity	_____	_____	_____
Running water	_____	_____	_____
Flush toilet	_____	_____	_____

	Now Have	Don't Have	Most Like to Have
Bathtub	_____	_____	_____
Hot water	_____	_____	_____
Central heating	_____	_____	_____
Refrigerator	_____	_____	_____
Clothes washer	_____	_____	_____
Clothes dryer	_____	_____	_____
Dishwasher	_____	_____	_____
Telephone	_____	_____	_____
TV set	_____	_____	_____
Other	XX	XX	_____
			(write in)
Not sure	XX	XX	_____

c. What's the first big improvement you'd make in your housing today? Anything else?

8a. In living in a neighborhood, if you could find the housing you want and like, would you rather live in a neighborhood with Negro families, or in a neighborhood that had both whites and Negroes?

Negroes	_____
Whites and Negroes	_____
Not sure	_____

b. Why do you feel this way?

9a. Do you feel that Negro children would do better or worse work if they all went to school along with white children today?

Better	_____
Worse	_____
About same (vol)	_____
Not sure	_____

10. Would you like to see all Negro children in your family go to school with white children or not?

Go with whites	_____
Not go with whites	_____
Not sure	_____

11a. Of course, because of where they live today, Negro children go to all Negro schools and whites to white schools. Would you like to see children in your family be picked up in buses every day so they could go to another part of town to go to school with white children or would that be too hard on the children?

Picked up by bus	_____
Too hard on children	_____
Not sure	_____

b. Have any young boys or girls in your family dropped out of high school?

Yes _____

No _____

c. Why do you think these young people are leaving school like that? Any other reason?

d. Well, do you think they ought to drop out of school like that if they want to, or do you think they ought to stay in school?

Ought to drop out
if want to _____
Ought to stay in _____
Not sure _____

e. All in all, do you feel your children (children in your family) are receiving as good an education as white children around here get, or are they getting not as good an education?

As good as whites _____
Inferior education _____
Not sure _____

f. Why do you feel this way? Any other reasons?

12a. Did you vote in the election for President in 1960 when Nixon and Kennedy ran?

Voted _____
Didn't vote _____

b. Did you vote in the election for President back in 1956, when Stevenson and Eisenhower ran?

Voted _____
Didn't vote _____

13a. Regardless of how you may vote, what do you usually consider yourself—a Republican, a Democrat, or what?

Republican _____
Democrat _____
Independent _____
Other

_____
(write in)
Not sure _____

14a. (IF VOTED IN 1960 IN Q. 12a) In 1960 for President, did you vote for Nixon, the Republican, or Kennedy, the Democrat?

Nixon   _____
Kennedy   _____
Can't recall   _____

b. (IF VOTED IN 1956 IN Q. 12b) In 1956 for President, did you vote for Stevenson, the Democrat, or Eisenhower, the Republican?

Stevenson   _____
Eisenhower   _____
Can't recall   _____

15a. Are you registered to vote now?

Yes   _____ (ASK Q. 15b)
No   _____ (SKIP TO d)

b. What are you registered as—a Democrat, a Republican, or what?

Democrat   _____
Republican   _____
Independent   _____
Other

_____
                (write in)
Not sure   _____

c. When did you first register to vote?

In past year   _____
1-2 years ago   _____
2-5 years ago   _____
Over 5 years ago   _____

d. (ASK EVERYONE) Are any (other) members of your family registered to vote?

Yes   _____
No   _____

e. (ASK ONLY IF NOT REGISTERED IN Q. 15a—OTHERWISE SKIP TO Q. 16a) Have you ever tried to register to vote?

Tried   _____ (SKIP TO g)
Not tried   _____ (ASK f)

f. What's the main reason you haven't tried to register to vote? Any other reason?

g. What happened when you tried to register to vote? How come you didn't get registered? Who kept you from registering to vote? How did they do that?

16a. In politics, do you feel Negroes should work mainly together as a separate group outside the two political parties or as individuals within one or the other party?

Mainly as a separate group _____
Mainly within parties _____
Both (vol) _____
Not sure _____

b. What's the main reason you feel that way?

17. Have you ever:

	Yes	No
1. Belonged to a political club or group	_____	_____
2. Worked for a political candidate for office	_____	_____
3. Asked people to register to vote	_____	_____
4. Asked people to vote for one candidate over another	_____	_____
5. Gone to a political meeting	_____	_____
6. Written or spoken to your congressman	_____	_____
7. Given money to a candidate or a political party	_____	_____

18a. Which party—the Republican or the Democratic—do you feel will do more to help Negroes in the next few years, or do you think there isn't much difference between the two?

Republican _____
Democratic _____
No difference _____
Not sure _____

b. What are the two or three main reasons you feel this way? Any others?

19a. What is your religion? What church do you attend?

Baptist _____
Methodist _____
Fundamentalist _____
Catholic _____
Other

_____
(write in)
No religion _____ (SKIP TO f)

b. How often do you go to church?

More than once a week	_____
Once a week	_____
Two or three times a month	_____
Once a month	_____
Less often	_____

c. Would you like to go to a church with all Negroes in it, or would you like to go to a church with whites and Negroes mixed together?

Mostly Negroes	_____
Whites and Negroes mixed together	_____
Not sure	_____

d. Do you feel that your church and your minister are helping a lot, some but not a lot, or only a little in working to get a better break for Negroes?

Helping a lot	_____
Some but not a lot	_____
Only a little	_____
Not at all	_____
Not sure	_____

e. Why do you say that? In what ways?

f. On the whole, do you approve or disapprove of the Black Muslim movement?

Approve	_____
Disapprove	_____
Not sure	_____

g. Why do you feel that way? Any other reasons?

20a. Have you stopped buying in certain stores in town because they won't hire Negroes?

Yes	_____ (ASK b)
No	_____ (SKIP TO c)

b. What stores are those? Any others? (Record name and type of store.)

c. Have you stopped buying certain companies' products because you have heard they discriminate against Negroes?

Yes	_____ (ASK d)
No	_____ (SKIP TO e)

d. What companies and products are those?

e. What chains or restaurants do you feel have fought the sit-ins the most and have refused the most to serve Negroes at lunch counters? Any others?

21a. Do you feel that bus riding for Negroes has improved in the past year or so, or is there not much change?

<blockquote>
Improved   _____
Not much change   _____
Not sure   _____
</blockquote>

b. Do you feel that railroad travel for Negroes has improved in the past year or so, or is there not much change?

<blockquote>
Improved   _____
Not much change   _____
Not sure   _____
</blockquote>

c. Do you feel the airlines discriminate against Negroes or not in travel accommodations?

<blockquote>
Yes, they do   _____
No, they don't   _____
Not sure   _____
</blockquote>

22a. What do you think is the best way to get movie theaters, restaurants, hotels and motels to admit and serve Negroes the same as they do whites—by passing a law in Congress, by carrying on picketing and sit-ins and sit-downs, or by getting white and Negro leaders to sit down with each other and agree to it? Which one, if you had to choose, will really make these things happen?

<blockquote>
Pass a law   _____
Demonstrate   _____
Leaders sit down together _____
None   _____
Not sure   _____
</blockquote>

b. Why did you say that?

23a. For most things you buy, do you feel you pay more than white people do for the same thing, less, or the same as whites?

<blockquote>
Pay more   _____
Pay less   _____
Pay same   _____
Not sure   _____
</blockquote>

b. Has this situation gotten better or worse in the past five years or hasn't it changed much?

Better	_____
Worse	_____
Not changed	_____
Not sure	_____

24a. In the cause of Negro rights, have you personally or has any member of your family:

b. If you were asked would you:

	a. Done	a. Not Done	b. Would	b. Would Not	b. Not Sure
Take(n) part in a sit-in	____	____	____	____	____
March(ed) in a demonstration	____	____	____	____	____
Picket(ed) a store	____	____	____	____	____
Stop(ped) buying at a store	____	____	____	____	____
Go(ne) to jail	____	____	____	____	____

c. What effect do you feel the demonstrations of Negroes all over the country have had up to now?

d. What effects do you feel the demonstrations will have in the future? Any other effects?

e. Do you see any dangers in the demonstrations? If so, what are they? Any others?

25a. Negro people all over have become much more active in the last few months. Why do you think Negro people have taken to direct action in the streets all over the country at this time? What's the main reason right now? Any others?

b. Have you personally felt different lately about your getting involved in direct action yourself?

Felt differently	_____ (ASK c)
Not felt differently	_____ ⎫ (SKIP TO d)
Not sure	_____ ⎭

c. How have you felt different? In what ways? Any other ways? What's happened in your own feelings and in your own life?

d. If you had to say how you feel, what would you personally like most to see change? What is it that you'd really most like to see done? Anything else?

e. Well, now, during your whole lifetime as far as you personally are concerned, if you had to name one thing, how has discrimination affected you the most? Anything else?

f. As far as all the things that have been going on lately with Negro rights, do you think things are moving about right these days, too fast, or too slow?

> About right _____
> Too fast _____
> Too slow _____
> Not sure _____

g. Why do you say that?

h. If the present demonstrations are successful, do you think in the next five years it will lead to a good deal of mixing of the races, some but not a lot, or only a little mixing of the races?

> A lot _____
> Some but not a lot _____
> Only a little _____
> Not sure _____

i. Would you actually personally like to see a lot of mixing of the races or would you just prefer that Negroes be treated like other members of the human race, even though there might not be a lot of mixing?

> Like lot of mixing _____
> Just treated like human
>   beings _____
> Not sure _____

j. Why do you feel this way? Any other reasons?

k. Some Negro leaders have proposed that whites and Negroes won't live well together, so the only solution is to set up a separate Negro state or states in this country or in Africa. Do you favor or oppose this idea?

> Favor _____
> Oppose _____
> Not sure _____

l. Why do you feel this way?

26a. Do you feel Negroes in the South are acting differently from Negroes in the North these days?

> Southern Negroes
>   different _____

Northern Negroes
different   _____
Nearly all the same   _____
Not sure   _____

b. Why do you say that? Any other reason?

27a. Do you feel the fact that Negroes originally came from Africa is an advantage or disadvantage?

Advantage   _____
Disadvantage   _____
Don't know   _____

b. Why?

28a. Some Negro leaders have said that Negroes can only succeed in winning rights if they use nonviolent means to demonstrate. Others disagree.

Do you personally feel Negroes today can win their rights without resorting to violence or do you think it will have to be an eye for an eye and a tooth for a tooth?

Can win without violence _____
Will have to use violence _____
Not sure   _____

b. Why do you believe this? Any other reasons?

29a. Some people have said that since there are 10 whites for every Negro in America, if it came to white against Negro, the Negroes would lose. Do you agree with this or disagree with it?

Agree   _____
Disagree   _____
Not sure   _____

b. Why do you feel this way?

c. What country of the world today do you feel is giving Negroes and other minorities the fairest break?

d. If the United States got into a war today would you personally feel this country was worth fighting for or not?

Worth fighting for   _____
Not worth it   _____
Not sure   _____

e. Why do you feel this way about fighting for this country? Any other reasons?

f. The Communists say under their system there's no discrimination. Do you believe that or not?

Believe   _____
Don't believe   _____
Not sure   _____

30a. If you had to choose one person or organization who has been most outstanding in the fight for Negro rights whom would you choose?

b. Why do you feel that way?

c. And what leader or organization do you think has let the Negro people down the most in the fight for Negro rights?

d. Why do you feel that way?

e. Now I want to read off to you a list of groups and people who have been prominent in the fight for Negro rights. For each I wish you would tell me how you would rate the job that person or group has done—excellent, pretty good, only fair, or poor?

	Excel-lent	Pretty Good	Only Fair	Poor	Not Sure
Floyd Patterson	___	___	___	___	___
Lena Horne	___	___	___	___	___
NAACP (National Association for the Advancement of Colored People)	___	___	___	___	___
Martin Luther King	___	___	___	___	___
CORE (Congress of Racial Equality)	___	___	___	___	___
Adam Clayton Powell	___	___	___	___	___
Elijah Muhammad	___	___	___	___	___
James Meredith	___	___	___	___	___
Harry Belafonte	___	___	___	___	___
National Urban League	___	___	___	___	___
SNCC (Student Nonviolent Co-ordinating Comm.)	___	___	___	___	___
Southern Christian Leadership Conference	___	___	___	___	___
Roy Wilkins	___	___	___	___	___
Ralph Bunche	___	___	___	___	___
Jackie Robinson	___	___	___	___	___
James Baldwin	___	___	___	___	___
Thurgood Marshall	___	___	___	___	___
Medgar Evers	___	___	___	___	___
Black Muslims	___	___	___	___	___
Dick Gregory	___	___	___	___	___

31a. Do you feel that the fight for Negroes' rights would be where it is today if the U.S. Supreme Court and the other courts had not passed their decisions or do you think what's happened would have taken place anyhow?

> Court decision very
> important _____
> Would have taken place _____
> Not sure _____

b. Why do you say that? Any other reasons?

32a. In the long run, would you count most in the fight for Negro rights on the courts, the Congress, or the President and the Executive branch?

> Courts _____
> Congress _____
> President _____
> None _____
> Not sure _____

b. Why do you feel this way? Any other reasons?

33a. If the election for President were being held today and if it were between Governor Nelson Rockefeller, the Republican, and President John F. Kennedy, the Democrat, and if you had to choose right now—would you vote for Rockefeller or for Kennedy?

> Rockefeller _____
> Kennedy _____
> Not sure _____

b. Suppose for President it were between Senator Barry Goldwater, the Republican, and President John F. Kennedy, the Democrat, who would you be for?

> Goldwater _____
> Kennedy _____
> Not sure _____

c. And if it were between Governor George Romney, the Republican, and President Kennedy, the Democrat, who would you be for?

> Romney _____
> Kennedy _____
> Not sure _____

34a. If President Kennedy wins re-election next year as President, do you think it will help Negro rights, set them back, or not change things much one way or the other?

Help Negro rights _____
Set them back _____
Not change things _____
Not sure _____

b. If President Kennedy loses re-election next year as President, do you think it will help Negro rights, set them back, or not change things much one way or the other?

Help Negro rights _____
Set them back _____
Not change things _____
Not sure _____

c. Which of the last four Presidents—Roosevelt, Truman, Eisenhower, or Kennedy—do you feel did the most for Negro rights in this country?

d. And which of the four did the least for Negro rights?

	c. Most	d. Least
Roosevelt	____	____
Truman	____	____
Eisenhower	____	____
Kennedy	____	____

e. (FOR MAN NAMED IN 34c) Why do you feel that way? Any other reasons?

35a. Now I want to give you a list of different people and groups that are run by white people. (HAND RESPONDENT WHITE CARD) (FOR EACH) Do you think (TAKE ONE AT A TIME ON CARD) has been more helpful or more harmful to Negro rights?

b. Now which of all these groups run by white people do you think has been most helpful to Negro rights?

c. And which has been most harmful to Negro rights?

	a. More Helpful	a. More Harmful	Not Sure	b. Most Helpful	c. Most Harmful
White churches	____	____	____	____	____
Labor unions	____	____	____	____	____
White businesses	____	____	____	____	____
Catholic priests	____	____	____	____	____
Jews	____	____	____	____	____
Bus companies	____	____	____	____	____
Hotels and motels	____	____	____	____	____

	a.			b.	c.
	More Help-ful	More Harm-ful	Not Sure	Most Help-ful	Most Harm-ful
Movie theaters	――	――	――	――	――
Real-estate companies	――	――	――	――	――
Federal government under Kennedy	――	――	――	――	――
Congress	――	――	――	――	――
U.S. Supreme Court	――	――	――	――	――
Local authorities	――	――	――	――	――
State government	――	――	――	――	――
Puerto Ricans	――	――	――	――	――

36a. On the whole, do you think most white people want to see Negroes get a better break, or do they want to keep Negroes down, or do you think they don't care one way or the other?

Better break   ――――

Keep down   ――――

Don't care one way or the other   ――――

Not sure   ――――

b. Why do you say that?

c. Do you think whites in the North care more about Negroes getting a better break than whites in the South, or do you think there isn't much difference?

North better than South ――――

Not much difference   ――――

Not sure   ――――

d. Why do you feel that way? Why do you think that's so? Any other reason?

e. What do you think is the main reason why some white people want to keep Negroes down? Any other reasons? What kind of people are they?

f. What about whites who want to see Negroes get ahead—why do you think they feel this way? Any other reason? What kind of people are they?

g. Compared to five years ago, do you think white people have changed their attitude about Negro rights for the better, for worse, or has there not been much change?

Better	_____
Worse	_____
Not much change	_____
Not sure	_____

h. Why do you feel this way? What's made it that way?

i. In the next five years, do you think the attitude of white people about Negro rights will get better, worse, or stay about the same?

Better	_____
Worse	_____
Stay the same	_____
Not sure	_____

j. Why do you think it will go that way?

k. In the end, do you think white people will take a better attitude toward Negroes mainly because they will be forced to by Negro action, or mainly because they can be persuaded that this is the only right thing to do?

Mainly force	_____
Mainly persuasion	_____
Not sure	_____

l. Why do you feel that way?

m. In both the South and North, there are some whites who are against the KKK and who want to see Negroes get a better break. But they also think that progress on Negro rights will not be as fast as Negro groups want. They are known as white moderates. On the whole, do you think these white moderates are more helpful or more harmful to Negro rights?

More helpful	_____
More harmful	_____
Not sure	_____

n. Why do you feel this way?

37a. What two or three white leaders and organizations do you respect and trust the most? Any others?

b. What two or three white leaders and organizations do you dislike and trust the least? Any others?

38a. How would you rate the job John F. Kennedy has done as President—excellent, pretty good, only fair, or poor?

Excellent	_____
Pretty good	_____

Only fair   ———
Poor   ———
Not sure   ———

b. What are the two or three main reasons you feel this way? Any other reasons?

39a. And how do you feel about the President's brother, Attorney General Robert Kennedy? How would you rate the job Robert Kennedy has done as Attorney General—excellent, pretty good, only fair, or poor?

Excellent   ———
Pretty good   ———
Only fair   ———
Poor   ———
Not sure   ———

b. Why do you feel this way? Any other reasons?

FACTUAL

40a. How old are you?

	Male	Female
18-20	———	———
21-34	———	———
35-49	———	———
50-59	———	———
60 and over	———	———

b. Are you currently married or single?

Married   ———
Single   ———
Widowed   ———
Separated or divorced   ———

c. How many children do you have 18 years of age or under?

One   ———
Two   ———
Three   ———
Four   ———
Five or more   ———
None   ———

d. How many are:

Under 2   ———
2-5   ———

6-10	_____
11-15	_____
16-18	_____

e. What is the last grade of school you completed? Also what was the last grade of school your father completed?

	Respondent	Father
2nd grade	_____	_____
3rd-4th grade	_____	_____
5th-8th grade	_____	_____
Some high school	_____	_____
Completed high school	_____	_____
Some college	_____	_____
Completed college	_____	_____
Graduate school	_____	_____

f. (IF COLLEGE) Which college did you attend? In what state is that?

g. What kind of job does (or did) your father have?

Professional	_____
Business	_____
Small business	_____
Labor, skilled	_____
Labor, unskilled	_____
Farmer	_____
Service, personal	_____
Government, civil serv.	_____
Office	_____
Transportation and Communications	_____

h. How many people in the family work?

One	_____
Two	_____
Three	_____
Four	_____
Five or more	_____
None	_____

i. Altogether how much do the people in your family who live here earn a week?

j. (IF EMPLOYED) How much do you earn a week?

$20	_____
$21-39	_____

$40-49 _____
$50-59 _____
$60-74 _____
$75-89 _____
$90-100 _____
$101-124 _____
$125-149 _____
$150-199 _____
$200 and over _____

41a. Are you a member of a labor union?

Yes _____ (SKIP TO c)
No _____ (ASK b)

b. Is any member of your family a member of a labor union?

Yes _____ (ASK c)
No _____ (SKIP TO d)

c. What union is that?

AFL-CIO _____
Teamsters _____
Other

_____
(write in)
Don't know _____

d. (IF MALE) Have you ever served in the armed forces?

Yes _____ (ASK e)
No _____ (SKIP TO g)

e. What branch?

Army _____
Navy _____
Air Force _____
Marines _____

f. Where were you stationed?

North _____
South _____
Overseas _____

g. How long have you lived in this state?

Less than a year _____
1-5 years _____
6-10 years _____

11-15 years _____
16-19 years _____
20 or more years _____

h. In what part of the country were you born and raised?

North _____
South _____
Midwest _____
West _____

i. What organizations are you a member of or active in?

j. Are you an officer in any organization(s)? Which one(s)?

42a. Do you (and your family) own a car?

Yes _____
No _____

b. Do you (and your family) own a television set?

Yes _____
No _____

c. Do you (and your family) own a radio?

Yes _____
No _____

d. (WHETHER OWNED OR NOT) How much time did you spend yesterday watching TV or listening to the radio?

	Television	Radio
None	_____	_____
1-30 minutes	_____	_____
31-59 minutes	_____	_____
More than 1 hour to less than 2 hours	_____	_____
More than 2 hours to less than 4 hours	_____	_____
More than 4 hours	_____	_____

e. Do you carry a life insurance policy?

Yes _____
No _____

f. Does anyone have a life insurance policy in your immediate family living here?

Yes _____
No _____

g. Do you have a bank's savings account or a checking account?

	Yes	No
Savings	_____	_____
Checking	_____	_____

h. Have you bought anything on the installment or credit plan in the last year?

Yes	_____
No	_____

i. (IF PRIVATE HOUSE OR CO-OP) Do you own or rent this house (Co-op)?

Own	_____
Rent	_____
Other	

_____
(specify)

j. How many rooms do you have?

One	_____
Two	_____
Three	_____
Four	_____
Five	_____
Six plus	_____

k. How many people, counting both adults and children, sleep and live here?

One	_____
Two-Three	_____
Four-Five	_____
Six-Seven	_____
Eight-Ten	_____
Ten and more	_____

APPENDIX **B**

SUPPLEMENTARY
STATISTICAL
TABLES

NOTE: This appendix contains tables not included in the text, as well as more detailed versions of tables summarized in the text. For convenient reference, the tables are grouped here in the order of the chapters to which they relate. Within each chapter group, the tables are then presented *according to the order of their subject matter as discussed in the text of that chapter*. Not every question from the questionnaire is represented by a table in this appendix (or in the text); but for those that are, the number of the relevant question is given in the upper left-hand corner. Some of the tables have, of course, been out-dated by the death of President John F. Kennedy in November 1963.

CHAPTER 3

QUESTION 25e

HOW DISCRIMINATION HAS AFFECTED NEGROES PERSONALLY

	Total Rank and File %	Total Non-South %	Total South %	Leaders %
Prevents my getting a job and wages I want—financial	30	34	27	26
Limited my education	11	11	11	13
Created inferiority complex—uneasy —resentment	7	7	7	22
Keeps me from going where want to —no freedom	6	4	8	4
Could not use public facilities	6	5	6	7
Received bad treatment—never treated like a man	5	3	6	10
Housing—couldn't get home where wanted to	3	5	2	1
Could not eat and be served	3	3	2	2
No ambition to further self—in job, education	2	2	1	8
Made me aware of my color—always judged by my color	2	3	2	3
Discriminated against in the service	*	1	—	2
Had no opportunities	*	*	—	1
Everyway—too many ways	2	2	2	1
All others	2	2	2	13
Has not affected me	13	14	12	4
Don't know	14	10	18	1

* Less than 1 per cent.

NOTE: Columns total more than 100% because some respondents named more than one experience of discrimination. Other tables in this appendix reflect a similar multiplicity of answers.

QUESTION 2c

JOBS HELD BY NEGROES

	Total Rank and File %	Total Non-South %	Total South %
LABOR			
Unskilled labor	16	19	14
Building trades	6	7	6
Janitor, sweeper	4	5	4
Transportation	4	4	4
Skilled factory	4	8	2
Other labor	3	2	3
PERSONAL SERVICE			
Waiter, domestic	12	8	14
Other personal service	4	4	6
WHITE COLLAR	5	7	4
PROFESSIONAL, EXECUTIVE			
Education	8	8	11
Other professional (M.D., clergy)	6	4	6
Businessman	2	2	3
OTHER	8	6	6
UNEMPLOYED	11	11	10
RETIRED, ON PENSION	7	5	7

FIELDS OF EMPLOYMENT IN WHICH NEGROES ARE GETTING BETTER BREAK

	Total Rank and File %	Total Non-South %	Total South %	Leaders %
Public jobs, local government	13	15	13	33
Social work, education	13	10	16	10
White collar, clerks, secretary	8	11	5	19
Civil service: office, clerical	6	8	5	12
Construction: crane operator, brick-layer	8	7	8	3
Doctors, dentists, lawyers, architects, clergy	5	6	5	19
Engineering	4	7	2	10
Factory labor, unskilled labor	5	4	6	7
Skilled labor, mechanics, plumber	3	3	4	5
Electronics	3	5	2	9
White collar, higher salesman, book-keeper, foreman	3	5	2	11
Nursing	4	4	4	1
Transportation: local and interstate (RR, bus, plane)	3	2	4	4
Small business: supermarket, grocery	2	2	2	4
Sports	3	3	3	3
Big industry, plants, large private industry and business	3	3	3	15
Hotel and restaurant: waiter, maid, domestic, waxer	2	2	2	1
Automotive trade: mechanic, car wash, repair, tires	2	1	2	—
Technicians	2	2	1	12
Business	2	2	1	2
Administrative, supervisory, executives, managers	1	1	1	4
Utilities: gas, water, power	1	1	1	—
Electricians	1	1	1	—
Military	1	1	*	—
Show business, music	1	2	1	1
Hospital labor	1	1	1	—
Personal service	1	*	1	—
Operatives	1	2	1	1
Labor unions	*	*	1	1
Elected government (politics)	1	*	1	1
All fields better	6	5	7	9
None	3	2	4	1
All fields bad	4	4	3	4
Don't know	22	21	22	3

* Less than 1 per cent.

FIELDS OF EMPLOYMENT IN WHICH NEGROES GET WORST BREAK

	Total Rank and File %	Total Non-South %	Total South %	Leaders %
Skilled labor	13	17	9	40
Construction: crane operator	10	15	7	38
White collar, clerks, secretary	12	13	12	11
Big industry, plants, large private industry and business	7	6	8	22
Electricians	7	10	5	12
Public jobs, local government	6	3	9	40
Administrative, supervisory, executives, managers	6	10	3	18
White collar, higher salesmen, bookkeeper, foreman	7	5	8	8
Transportation: local and interstate (RR, bus, plane)	6	6	6	9
Factory labor, unskilled labor	5	6	4	5
Small business: supermarket, grocery, small retail store	6	3	7	1
Business	3	4	3	4
Labor unions	2	4	1	23
Civil service: post office, police	4	3	5	2
Engineering	5	5	4	1
Doctors, dentists, lawyers, clergy	3	5	2	3
Operatives	3	4	2	3
Utilities: gas, water, power	3	3	3	1
Hotel and restaurant: waiter, maid, domestic, waxer	3	*	4	1
Technician	2	2	1	2
Electronics	1	1	1	—
Civil service: office, clerical	1	*	1	2
Elected government (politics)	1	2	*	1
Communications	1	*	1	2
Automotive trade: mechanic, car wash, repair, tires	1	2	1	—
Social work, education	2	2	1	1
Show business, music	1	1	—	4
Sports	*	—	*	—
Military	*	—	*	—
Hospital labor	*	*	*	—
Nursing	*	*	1	—
Personal services	*	*	*	—
None	*	—	1	—
All fields bad	8	8	8	5
Don't know	25	21	28	4

* Less than 1 per cent.

QUESTION 3c

NEGROES ASSESS CHANCES OF EQUAL PAY
FOR EQUAL WORK

	Total Rank and File %		NON-SOUTH				SOUTH			
		Total Non-South %	Low Income %	Lower Middle Income %	Middle and Upper Income %	Total South %	Urban %	Non-Urban %	Middle and Upper Income %	Leaders %
Would get same pay as whites	33	43	31	42	55	25	25	22	43	43
Less pay	56	47	63	48	36	63	63	66	48	48
Not sure	11	10	6	10	9	12	12	12	9	9

QUESTION 41a

NEGRO LABOR UNION MEMBERSHIP

	Total Rank and File %	Total Non-South %	Total South %	Leaders %
Member of union	19	28	11	17
Not a member	81	72	89	83

QUESTION 11b

HIGH-SCHOOL DROPOUTS IN FAMILY

	Total All Interviews %	Total Rank and File %	Total Non-South %	Total South %	Leaders %
Have had dropouts in family	19	20	17	21	10
No dropouts in family	81	80	83	79	90

QUESTION 11d

ATTITUDES TOWARD SCHOOL DROPOUTS

	Total Rank and File %	Total Non-South %	Total South %	Leaders %
Ought to drop out if want to	1	2	1	4
Ought to stay in	99	98	99	96

QUESTION 11f

WHY EDUCATION OF NEGRO CHILDREN IS AS GOOD AS OR INFERIOR TO THAT OF WHITE CHILDREN

	Total Rank and File %	Total Non-South %	Total South %
As GOOD AS WHITES			
Go to mixed, integrated school	9	17	3
Get same, equal chance, taught same	9	13	7
Have good, qualified teachers	5	4	5
Have new, improved system	4	4	3
If child motivated, can learn	4	5	4
Use private, parochial schools	2	2	2
Just Negro area, no whites	1	*	1
No problems, no trouble	1	2	*
INFERIOR TO WHITES			
Facilities, equipment, opportunities inferior to those of whites	19	8	28
Don't give same work	11	11	11
Textbooks not as good, not up to date	6	2	9
Discriminate, don't treat fairly	6	9	4
Inferior school buildings	6	5	7
Pains not taken with Negro child	5	6	5
Not getting all subjects	3	1	5
Parents don't care enough	2	2	2
Segregated, inferior	2	2	2
NOT SURE	19	20	17

* Less than 1 per cent.

QUESTION 7a

FACILITIES NEGROES HAVE IN THEIR HOMES

		NON-SOUTH				SOUTH				
	Total Rank and File %	Total Non-South %	Low Income %	Lower Middle Income %	Middle and Upper Income %	Total South %	Urban %	Non-Urban %	Middle and Upper Income %	Leaders %
NOW HAVE:										
Electricity	99	100	100	100	100	98	99	96	100	100
Refrigerator	97	98	81	98	100	96	98	94	100	99
TV set	92	95	75	95	100	89	87	85	97	100
Running water	92	99	94	100	100	86	97	69	100	100
Inside toilet	89	99	81	100	100	82	96	60	100	100
Flush toilet	89	99	81	100	100	82	96	59	100	100
Bathtub	88	96	31	99	100	80	93	59	100	100
Hot water	86	98	38	100	100	76	87	57	100	100
Clothes washer	61	63	44	62	81	58	54	60	81	84
Central heating	60	89	21	90	98	38	41	22	91	93
Telephone	71	80	37	79	100	65	69	54	100	100
Clothes dryer	14	17	—	15	37	10	9	5	40	57
Dishwasher	5	6	—	5	19	5	4	3	25	49

QUESTION 4

NEGROES ASSESS RENTS THEY WOULD HAVE TO PAY COMPARED TO WHITES FOR SAME ACCOMMODATIONS

	Total Rank and File %	NON-SOUTH				SOUTH				
		Total Non-South %	Low Income %	Lower Middle Income %	Middle and Upper Income %	Total South %	Urban %	Non-Urban %	Middle and Upper Income %	Leaders %
Same	30	21	19	21	14	37	37	41	28	20
More	53	68	62	68	84	41	40	35	66	76
Not sure	17	11	19	11	2	22	23	24	6	4

QUESTION 23a

NEGROES ASSESS PRICES THEY PAY COMPARED WITH WHITES FOR SAME THINGS

	Total Rank and File %	Total Non-South %	SOUTH				
			Total South %	Urban %	Non-Urban %	Middle and Upper Income %	Leaders %
Pay more	19	23	16	15	18	9	13
Pay less	2	2	2	2	2	—	1
Pay same	70	69	71	70	70	91	86
Not sure	9	6	11	13	10	—	—

QUESTION 29c

COUNTRY NEGROES FEEL TREATS THEM AND OTHER MINORITIES MOST FAIRLY

	Total Rank and File %	Leaders %
United States	21	31
France	5	8
Africa	2	8
England	3	1
Canada	1	1
Practically any country	1	—
European countries	1	1
Italy	1	—
Scandinavia	1	8
Germany	1	—
Switzerland	1	2
West Indies	1	1
Japan	1	1
Mexico	1	—
Brazil	*	7
Russia	1	1
South America	1	—
All but USA	*	—
India	*	1
Any except USA and S. Africa	*	—
Not the USA	*	—
None	4	1
All others	5	9
Don't know	51	28

* Less than 1 per cent.

QUESTION 29d

NEGRO WILLINGNESS TO FIGHT FOR THE U.S.A.

	Total Rank and File %	Non-South Low Income %	Leaders %
Worth fighting for	81	81	91
Not worth it	9	13	5
Not sure	10	6	4

QUESTION 29a

WHY NEGROES FEEL UNITED STATES IS OR IS NOT WORTH FIGHTING FOR

	Total Rank and File %	Total Non-South %	Total South %	Leaders %
WORTH FIGHTING FOR:				
It's home, don't know any other country, I was born here	31	33	29	18
This is my country (as well as whites')	21	23	20	17
Worth fighting for	7	6	7	12
I am an American citizen	6	5	7	16
I live in this country, it's worth it	5	5	6	14
Every man should fight for his country	5	5	4	4
This is a great country, room for everyone	3	4	1	11
Because of my family and my people	2	2	2	3
I have grievance but I would fight	1	1	—	—
We do have a little freedom here	1	1	*	2
If you are not free here you are not free anywhere	*	*	*	—
All other positive	26	24	27	46
NOT WORTH IT:				
We don't have equal rights here	3	3	3	4
Not worth it	1	1	1	—
American flag doesn't represent us	1	1	1	—
Why fight for the white man?	1	1	1	1
Why fight for a country that doesn't fight for Negroes?	2	2	1	—
In world we are American, in United States we are Negroes —"Why fight?"	1	1	1	—
Not the way things are now	1	1	1	—
To die for my country means nothing	*	*	—	—
All other not worth it	2	2	3	—
DON'T KNOW	6	3	8	1

* Less than 1 per cent.

QUESTION 29f

NEGROES ASSESS CREDIBILITY OF COMMUNIST CLAIM OF NO DISCRIMINATION UNDER THEIR SYSTEM

	Total Rank and File %	Non-South %	South %	Leaders %
Believe	5	4	6	2
Don't believe	58	63	55	88
Not sure	37	33	39	10

CHAPTER 4

QUESTION 24c

NEGROES ASSESS EFFECTS OF DEMONSTRATIONS

	Total Rank and File %	Total Non-South %	Total South %	Leaders %
Do some good—help situation—get results	33	32	33	15
Bring awareness of their situation, condition to country	18	20	15	63
Awaken whites	12	14	10	17
Integration—opening up	7	7	7	5
Show determination to fight for what belongs to him	7	7	7	9
Obtain equal rights	5	5	5	3
Help Negro to achieve objectives	3	2	4	—
Unity of purpose, oneness of people	3	4	2	7
Stirred people up—action	2	2	2	5
Get freedom	1	1	1	—
Schools integrated	1	2	1	1
Civil rights, laws	1	1	1	4
Push South Negroes to thinking—will vote	*	*	*	—
Do some good if there is no violence	*	*	—	1
All other positive	*	*	*	—
Antipathy of whites, tension	1	1	1	1
Jail	*	*	1	1
Violence, loss of lives, bloodshed, rioting	2	3	1	2
All other negative	2	1	2	1
None, too much	4	4	4	—
Don't know	14	11	17	—

* Less than 1 per cent.

QUESTION 24a

NEGRO PARTICIPATION IN DIRECT ACTION

	Total Rank and File %	Total Non-South %	Low Income %	Lower Middle Income %	Middle and Upper Income %	Total South %	Urban %	Non-Urban %	Middle and Upper Income %	Leaders %
		NON-SOUTH					SOUTH			
Stopped buying at a store	33	28	6	25	63	38	43	21	79	70
Marched in a demonstration	12	14	13	10	44	11	11	7	30	62
Picketed a store	9	9	6	7	23	10	10	5	30	54
Taken part in a sit-in	8	7	13	6	12	9	7	6	28	39
Gone to jail	4	3	—	3	2	6	6	4	15	21

QUESTION 24b

NEGRO WILLINGNESS TO PARTICIPATE IN DIRECT ACTION

	Total Rank and File %	Total Non-South %	Low Income %	Lower Middle Income %	Middle and Upper Income %	Total South %	Urban %	Non-Urban %	Middle and Upper Income %	Leaders %
		NON-SOUTH					SOUTH			
IF ASKED, I WOULD:										
March in a demonstration	51	60	63	59	67	44	43	43	53	57
Take part in a sit-in	49	59	63	59	58	42	41	44	45	57
Go to jail	47	52	56	51	63	43	44	41	47	58
Picket a store	46	54	44	54	58	40	38	39	51	57

QUESTION 25b

CHANGE IN NEGRO FEELING ABOUT PARTICIPATION IN DIRECT ACTION

	Total Rank and File %	Non-South %	South %	Leaders %
Felt different lately	32	37	27	42
Not felt different	50	47	53	57
Not sure	18	16	20	1

QUESTION 25c

HOW FELT DIFFERENT ABOUT PERSONAL INVOLVEMENT

	Total Rank and File %	Non-South %	South %	Leaders %
My duty to help, we should all be in it	46	50	43	27
More consciousness to improve, want betterment	23	23	24	46
Have joined organization to work together	9	5	13	19
When I see my people mistreated	9	9	10	8
Want to fight for equal rights	8	8	8	—
Not sure	5	5	6	—

QUESTION 20a

NEGRO BOYCOTT OF STORES BECAUSE OF DISCRIMINATORY HIRING

	Total Rank and File %	NON-SOUTH		SOUTH		Leaders %
		Total Non-South %	Middle and Upper Income %	Total South %	Middle and Upper Income %	
Have stopped buying in certain stores because of discriminatory hiring	28	24	54	30	60	55
Have not stopped buying	72	76	46	70	40	45

QUESTION 20c

EXTENT OF NEGRO BOYCOTT OF PRODUCTS FROM COMPANIES THAT DISCRIMINATE

| | NON-SOUTH | | | SOUTH | | |
	Total Rank and File %	Total Non-South %	Middle and Upper Income %	Total South %	Middle and Upper Income %	Leaders %
Have boycotted	16	14	37	18	58	52
Have not boycotted	84	86	63	82	42	48

QUESTION 24e

DANGERS NEGROES SEE IN DEMONSTRATIONS

	Total Rank and File %	Total Non-South %	Total South %	Leaders %
Violence, bloodshed, loss of life and property, danger	50	52	49	73
Dogs, water hoses, police brutality	5	5	5	4
Negroes being hurt physically	5	4	5	3
None as long as they remain non-violent	4	4	4	5
Riot—out of hand	3	3	3	2
Causes conflict, rebellion, civil war	1	1	2	4
Death of leaders, murder	2	3	2	1
Jailed	1	1	1	—
Tension, hatred	1	1	1	—
Not in North, but in South there will be danger	1	2	*	1
Could be misunderstood, demonstration considered threat	*	*	*	—
All others	2	1	2	—
None	26	28	26	9
Don't know	5	4	6	—

* Less than 1 per cent.

WHY NEGROES FEEL THEY CAN WIN WITH OR WITHOUT RESORTING TO VIOLENCE

	Total Rank and File %	NON-SOUTH				Total South %	SOUTH			
		Total Non-South %	Low Income %	Lower Middle Income %	Middle and Upper Income %		Urban %	Non-Urban %	Middle and Upper Income %	Leaders %
WITHOUT VIOLENCE										
Don't favor violence, nonviolence, best solution, don't want to hurt people	34	34	19	33	47	34	31	36	45	64
Will gain more by nonviolence, can win by non-violence	14	16	6	15	23	13	14	11	19	10
Don't need violence—God is on our side, prayers best	4	4	6	4	2	5	5	5	2	2
Better to talk than to fight, peaceful demonstrations best	4	4	13	4	—	3	3	2	6	3
Democratic form of government will achieve our aims; Kennedy will solve problem	3	4	—	4	—	3	4	1	6	5
Favorable public opinion is better than violence	1	1	—	1	2	2	1	2	2	1
Good leadership	1	1	—	1	—	1	1	1	—	1
Other reasons	3	3	6	3	5	3	3	1	6	8

WHY NEGROES FEEL THEY CAN WIN WITH OR WITHOUT RESORTING TO VIOLENCE

	Total Rank and File %	NON-SOUTH				SOUTH				
		Total Non-South %	Low Income %	Lower Middle Income %	Middle and Upper Income %	Total South %	Urban %	Non-Urban %	Middle and Upper Income %	Leaders %
WITH VIOLENCE										
Only resort—all that's left, must fight back, won't take any more	12	12	13	12	7	12	14	12	—	1
May have to resort to violence	5	6	6	6	5	5	4	5	9	8
Use force if necessary	3	3	13	2	5	3	3	1	2	3
Violence for defense	2	4	—	4	5	1	1	1	—	3
Eye for eye, tooth for tooth	1	2	—	3	—	1	—	1	2	1
Can't win peacefully, nonviolence has failed	1	1	—	1	—	1	1	*	—	1
Have to do something	*	*	—	1	—	*	—	—	2	—
Other reasons	2	2	—	3	—	2	2	1	6	2
DON'T KNOW	12	9	19	10	4	15	13	20	—	—

* Less than 1 per cent.

QUESTION 29b

WHY NEGROES FEEL THEY WOULD OR WOULD NOT LOSE IN A SHOWDOWN WITH WHITES

	Total Rank and File %	NON-SOUTH				SOUTH				
		Total Non-South %	Low Income %	Lower Middle Income %	Middle and Upper Income %	Total South %	Urban %	Non-Urban %	Middle and Upper Income %	Leaders %
WOULD LOSE										
Whites have power, policemen, could kill us all, they have guns	13	11	13	11	19	13	16	8	26	14
Odds are too great, don't stand chance, we're minority, 10% not enough	9	9	13	9	12	10	10	6	26	31
White man will aid, need the Negro	8	9	6	8	26	7	7	5	17	10
People have too much sense for this	3	3	—	3	2	4	2	3	13	9
Agree	1	1	—	1	—	1	1	1	—	3
Religion is help, religion says nonviolence is best	1	1	—	1	2	1	1	2	—	1
Federal government will have to defend Negro	1	*	—	1	—	1	1	—	—	1
We lose everything anyway	1	*	—	1	—	1	1	—	—	—
All others	3	4	—	4	9	2	1	2	2	17

WHY NEGROES FEEL THEY WOULD OR WOULD NOT LOSE IN A SHOWDOWN WITH WHITES

	Total Rank and File %	NON-SOUTH				SOUTH				
		Total Non-South %	Low Income %	Lower Middle Income %	Middle and Upper Income %	Total South %	Urban %	Non-Urban %	Middle and Upper Income %	Leaders %
WOULD NOT LOSE										
Negroes best, better fighters	20	19	25	20	5	21	22	23	2	2
Statistics are wrong	4	5	—	5	5	3	3	3	—	3
God is on our side	3	2	13	2	—	3	4	3	—	1
Makes no difference	3	3	—	3	2	3	3	1	4	1
Disagree	2	3	6	3	—	2	3	*	—	—
There are more Negroes, outnumber whites	2	2	—	3	—	1	2	1	—	1
Have to do something	1	1	—	1	—	1	1	*	4	3
Right will always win	1	1	—	2	—	1	1	*	—	—
Depends	1	1	—	1	5	1	1	1	—	1
DON'T KNOW	23	25	24	24	17	25	21	42	16	5

* Less than 1 per cent.

QUESTION 22a

NEGROES ASSESS TACTICS MOST LIKELY TO BRING THEM ADMISSION TO PUBLIC ACCOMMODATIONS

	Total Rank and File %	Total Non-South %	Total South %	Leaders %
Pass a law	39	44	34	42
Demonstrate	8	9	8	15
White and Negro leaders sit down together	41	38	43	40
None	1	1	1	1
Not sure	11	8	14	2

QUESTION 32a

IN FIGHT FOR THEIR RIGHTS, NEGROES CHOOSE BETWEEN THE COURTS, CONGRESS, OR PRESIDENT FOR MOST HELP

	Total Rank and File %	Leaders %
Courts	26	56
Congress	12	11
President	44	26
None	2	2
Not sure	16	5

QUESTION 32b

WHY NEGROES WOULD MOST COUNT ON THE COURTS, CONGRESS, OR THE KENNEDY ADMINISTRATION IN THE FIGHT FOR THEIR RIGHTS

	Total Rank and File %	Total Non-South %	Total South %	Leaders %
COURTS				
Enforced the law	7	6	9	15
Respected, decision carries weight, effective	7	7	8	13
Courts most important	4	3	4	5
Fair, just, neutral	3	3	3	10
Reliable	2	1	2	9
Started ball rolling	2	2	2	4
All other courts	1	1	1	8
CONGRESS				
They make the laws	6	8	5	2
Congress most important	2	1	2	3
Has more power	1	2	1	1
President can't move without Congress	1	1	1	—
All other Congress	*	1	*	1
PRESIDENT KENNEDY				
Doing something, done a lot	9	8	10	1
Has necessary power to get things done	8	10	6	9
Leader of the nation	8	9	7	6
More for the Negro	6	6	7	—
President most important	4	2	5	2
Took a firm stand for equal rights and opportunity	4	6	4	2
Must enforce the laws	3	3	3	1
Must initiate action, legislation	4	3	4	2
All other President Kennedy	*	1	*	1
NONE	1	2	1	2
ALL SAME	5	7	3	7
DON'T KNOW	15	14	17	5

* Less than 1 per cent.

CHAPTER 5

QUESTION 15c

WHEN FIRST REGISTERED TO VOTE

	Total Rank and File %	Total Non-South %	Total South %
In past year	4	4	5
1–2 years ago	4	2	7
2–5 years ago	12	11	13
Over 5 years ago	80	83	75

QUESTION 13a

POLITICAL ORIENTATION

	Total Rank and File %	Total Non-South %	Total South %	Leaders %
Democratic	74	77	71	55
Republican	11	10	12	20
Independent	14	12	16	23
Other	1	1	1	2

QUESTION 18a

WHICH PARTY WILL DO MORE FOR NEGROES IN NEXT FEW YEARS

	Total Rank and File %	Leaders %
Democratic	64	63
Republican	4	4
No difference	18	29
Not sure	14	4

QUESTION 18b

WHY FEEL REPUBLICAN OR DEMOCRATIC PARTY WILL DO MORE TO HELP NEGROES

	Total Rank and File %	Total Non-South %	Total South %	Leaders %
DEMOCRATS WILL DO MORE				
Past record on Negro better	28	26	29	18
For the poor, little man	12	13	11	27
President Kennedy and Administration doing a lot	14	11	16	11
Done most on laws for Negroes	7	7	7	12
Good on integration, civil rights	6	5	7	4
Better on jobs	5	4	5	3
Always been a Democrat	4	6	2	2
Housing good	1	1	1	—
Education good	1	1	1	2
More responsive to Negro pressure	—	—	—	8
REPUBLICANS WILL DO MORE				
Traditionally best for Negro	3	2	3	3
Done most for Negroes	1	*	2	2
NO DIFFERENCE				
Neither will help much	12	17	7	15
Depends on man, not party	4	4	4	4
Time, not party, will cause change	2	2	2	12
NOT SURE	18	13	22	3

* Less than 1 per cent.

QUESTIONS 34c, d

ASSESSMENT OF LAST FOUR PRESIDENTS ON NEGRO RIGHTS

	Total Rank and File %	Total Non-South %	Total South %	Leaders %
DID MOST FOR NEGRO RIGHTS				
Kennedy	73	62	80	49
Roosevelt	20	30	13	15
Eisenhower	4	4	5	10
Truman	3	4	2	26
DID LEAST FOR NEGRO RIGHTS				
Eisenhower	48	53	45	63
Truman	34	31	35	10
Roosevelt	8	7	10	14
Kennedy	*	—	1	1
Not sure	10	9	9	12

    * Less than 1 per cent.

QUESTION 38a

PRESIDENT KENNEDY JOB RATING

	Total Rank and File %	Total Non-South %	Total South %	Leaders %
Excellent	62	54	70	29
Pretty good	27	34	23	55
Only fair	7	10	4	15
Poor	1	1	—	1
Not sure	3	1	3	—

QUESTION 38b

REASONS FOR PRESIDENT KENNEDY
JOB RATING

	Total Rank and File %	Total Non-South %	Total South %	Leaders %
POSITIVE				
NEGRO RIGHTS				
Helping the Negro, knows problems	18	13	22	8
Helping Negroes on new laws	12	11	13	13
Speaks out for Negroes	8	10	6	1
For jobs, fair job rights	8	5	9	3
Firm stand on Negro rights	6	6	5	8
For education for Negroes	4	3	5	—
Given Negroes top jobs in government	3	3	3	1
Enforced Supreme Court ruling	3	3	3	—
Sent troops to Mississippi	2	2	2	4
No discrimination in government	1	—	1	—
Help on Negro housing	1	1	1	2
DOING BEST HE CAN	26	24	28	20
APPEALING MAN				
Sincere, honest, keeps promises	4	4	4	3
Good man, like him	4	3	4	—
Speaks well on TV	3	3	2	8
Courage of convictions	3	3	3	8
Speaks out for right	3	3	2	2
Religious, churchgoing	1	*	1	—
GOOD ON FOREIGN AFFAIRS	5	5	6	15
NEGATIVE				
TOO SLOW, RELUCTANT ON NEGRO RIGHTS	10	13	7	29
NOT FAMILIAR WITH HIM	5	2	6	7

* Less than 1 per cent.

QUESTIONS 34a, b

EFFECT ON NEGRO RIGHTS OF 1964 KENNEDY RE-ELECTION OR DEFEAT

	Total Rank and File %	Total Non-South %	Total South %	Leaders %
KENNEDY RE-ELECTION WILL:				
Help Negro rights	82	76	87	79
Set rights back	1	2	1	—
Not change things	9	12	6	14
Not sure	8	10	6	7
KENNEDY DEFEAT WILL:				
Help Negro rights	3	4	3	3
Set them back	42	42	43	42
Not change things	31	34	29	28
Not sure	24	20	25	27

QUESTION 39a

ATTORNEY GENERAL ROBERT KENNEDY JOB RATING

	Total Rank and File %	Total Non-South %	Total South %	Leaders %
Excellent	55	49	62	57
Pretty good	27	34	22	35
Only fair	7	8	6	5
Poor	1	1	—	2
Not sure	10	8	10	1

QUESTION 39b

REASONS FOR ROBERT KENNEDY JOB RATING

	Total Rank and File %	Total Non-South %	Total South %	Leaders %
POSITIVE				
Works hard to carry out justice	28	28	29	32
Works with JFK to help race	13	10	15	5
Good job	11	9	13	12
Outspoken, speaks his mind	10	11	9	11
Stood behind his beliefs and words	7	7	7	14
Protected Meredith with troops	4	5	4	2
Visited troubled areas	3	4	2	3
Shown action throughout South	2	3	—	1
Knows more about rights than JFK	1	1	1	5
Devoted much time to Negro	1	1	1	2
Increased Negro job opportunities	1	—	2	2
Helping Negroes get the vote	1	—	1	3
Talking with white leaders	1	1	—	—
NEGATIVE				
Worked on rights only when forced to	5	5	3	15
NOT FAMILIAR WITH HIM	15	14	16	4

QUESTIONS 33a, b, c

HOW NEGROES WOULD VOTE IN 1964 PRESIDENTIAL RACE

	Total Rank and File %	Total Non-South %	Total South %	Leaders %
KENNEDY VS. ROCKEFELLER				
Kennedy	89	86	91	68
Rockefeller	3	4	3	21
Not sure	8	10	6	11
KENNEDY VS. GOLDWATER				
Kennedy	91	91	92	92
Goldwater	2	2	2	3
Not sure	7	7	6	5
KENNEDY VS. ROMNEY				
Kennedy	89	87	90	84
Romney	3	4	2	5
Not sure	8	9	8	11

QUESTION 16a

NEGROES IN POLITICS: SHOULD WORK AS SEPARATE GROUP OR AS INDIVIDUALS WITHIN EXISTING POLITICAL PARTIES

	Total Rank and File %	Leaders %
Mainly as separate group	9	7
Mainly within existing parties	67	67
Both	8	23
Not sure	16	3

QUESTION 16b

WHY NEGROES SHOULD WORK SEPARATELY OR WITHIN POLITICAL PARTIES

	Total Rank and File %	Leaders %
SEPARATE GROUP		
Can accomplish more	4	1
Strength in unity	3	7
Parties won't help Negro	1	—
BOTH		
Can accomplish more, have more power	4	8
Help to understand, work together	3	10
WITHIN PARTIES		
Accomplish more	16	12
All work together, all the same	13	11
Shouldn't segregate ourselves	8	11
Results in better understanding, unity, cooperation	6	2
Can work for your choice of parties	4	7
More power	4	9
Best, better	4	7
Can know what's going on	3	2
Can help choose best candidate	2	6
Each person should have own opinion, be independent	3	4
Separate party no good	2	7
Parties will have more interest in Negro	1	7
NOT SURE	19	3

CHAPTER 6

QUESTION 19a

NEGRO RELIGIOUS DENOMINATIONS

	Total Rank and File %	Total Non-South %	Total South %	Leaders %
Baptist	55	52	58	28
Methodist	18	18	18	25
Fundamentalist	7	6	8	1
Catholic	7	7	6	3
Other Protestant	10	13	7	35
No religion	3	4	3	8

QUESTION 19b

HOW OFTEN NEGROES GO TO CHURCH

	Total all Interviews %	Total Rank and File %	Total Non-South %	Total South %	Leaders %
More than once a week	20	20	17	22	24
Once a week	29	29	28	30	24
Two or three times a month	24	25	22	27	16
Once a month	10	10	10	10	9
Less often	17	16	23	11	27

QUESTION 19d

NEGRO ASSESSES EXTENT TO WHICH HIS MINISTER AND CHURCH ARE ASSISTING CAUSE

	Total all Inter- views %	Total Rank and File %	Total Non- South %	Total South %	Leaders %
Helping a Lot	47	47	48	45	48
Some, but not a lot	17	16	15	18	25
Only a little	12	12	10	13	14
Not at all	5	5	5	5	6
Not sure	19	20	22	19	7

QUESTION 19e

WHY NEGRO FEELS AS HE DOES ABOUT ROLE OF HIS MINISTER AND CHURCH IN CAUSE

	Total all Inter- views %	Total Rank and File %	Total Non- South %	Total South %	Leaders %
MINISTER HELPING					
Teaches equality, brotherhood of man	16	16	15	18	8
Working actively on better equal race relations	14	12	14	11	29
They are working, helping, offering help	10	11	8	13	8
Keep the people informed	5	6	6	5	—
They are the Negro spokesman	5	4	4	5	9
Encourages cooperation and working with groups (NAACP)	5	5	6	4	4
Doing a good job	3	3	4	3	7
Helps church members get jobs	2	2	3	1	—
Preaches equal job opportunities for all	2	2	4	1	1
Organizes demonstrations	1	1	1	1	1
Preach cooperation, peaceful methods, nonviolence	1	1	1	1	—
Catholic churches are integrated	1	1	1	1	—
All other positive	24	23	23	23	41
MINISTER NOT HELPING					
Not done much, not effective, could do more	6	6	6	6	13
Our minister not interested	5	5	4	5	1
People in my church not doing much	2	2	1	3	1
Some ministers just interested in money	1	1	1	*	1
Christianity, religion important	1	1	1	1	—
Some ministers prejudiced	*	*	*	—	1
All other negative	3	3	4	2	1
DON'T KNOW	20	21	22	21	9

* Less than 1 per cent.

QUESTION 19c

NEGRO ATTITUDE ON INTEGRATED CHURCHES

	Total Rank and File %	Total Non-South %	Total South %	Leaders %
WOULD LIKE TO GO TO CHURCH WITH:				
Mostly Negroes	22	18	26	9
Whites, Negroes mixed	52	58	47	73
Not sure	26	24	27	18

CHAPTER 7

QUESTION 26a

DIFFERENCE IN BEHAVIOR BETWEEN SOUTHERN AND NORTHERN NEGROES RECENTLY

	Total Rank and File %	Non-South %	South %	Leaders %
Southern Negroes acting different from Northern	37	52	26	60
Northern Negroes acting different from Southern	7	2	10	33
Nearly all the same	39	33	43	4
Not sure	17	13	21	3

QUESTION 26b

WHY NEGROES ARE ACTING DIFFERENT IN NORTH OR SOUTH

	Total Rank and File %	Non-South %	South %	Leaders %
WHY SOUTHERN NEGROES ACTING DIFFERENT FROM NORTHERN				
Fighting, more militant for rights	14	24	7	44
South kept under more pressure	14	18	11	18
South started demonstrations	2	3	2	4
More afraid of white people	2	2	2	—
Have less education	1	—	1	—
Have unity, strength	1	2	1	1
Tired of being pushed around	1	1	—	—
Have fewer job opportunities	1	1	1	—
WHY NORTHERN NEGROES ACTING DIFFERENT FROM SOUTHERN				
Have more rights like whites	5	2	8	—
More educated	1	1	1	—
Live better, jobs, wages	1	—	1	—
WHY NEARLY ALL SAME	13	12	13	14
All want equal rights, chances				
See us different, act no different	10	7	11	5
Discrimination causes demonstrations in both places	7	7	7	11
Many Negroes in both places have moved back and forth	2	1	2	1
All want good treatment	1	2	1	1
NOT SURE	24	17	31	1

QUESTION 19f

ATTITUDE TOWARD BLACK MUSLIM MOVEMENT

	Total Rank and File %	Non-South %	South %	Leaders %
Approve	6	9	3	8
Disapprove	51	59	48	84
Not sure	43	32	49	8

QUESTION 19g

WHY DISAPPROVE OR APPROVE OF MUSLIMS

	Total Rank and File %	Non-South %	South %	Leaders %
WHY DISAPPROVE				
Hatred not needed now, wrong to hate	12	15	10	27
Don't need a race division	5	8	2	25
Any racial supremacy wrong	5	4	6	17
Want to stay an American, no other	4	5	2	3
Mixed feelings	4	6	2	11
They don't believe in God	2	5	1	2
They're fighting against Negroes	2	2	1	1
Hindering, not helping us	1	2	1	—
Every man entitled to his own religion	1	2	1	—
Other reasons	3	5	2	—
APPROVE				
Trying to improve Negroes as people	6	9	3	8
NOT SURE	55	37	69	6

QUESTION 251

WHY OPPOSE OR FAVOR SEPARATE STATE FOR NEGROES IN U.S. OR AFRICA

	Total Rank and File %	Non-South %	South %	Leaders %
WHY OPPOSE				
People should live in harmony	23	23	23	19
We are Americans; this is our home	19	17	21	18
Don't believe in separation—will not solve problem	17	22	13	32
Don't want to go to Africa	6	5	6	4
Created equal to whites, should be part of U.S.	4	5	4	9
Fighting to be part of U.S.—don't want to leave	3	5	3	4
Negro fought for, worked, helped build country	3	3	2	1
People should have choice of where want to live	3	4	3	3
Have to live for each other	3	1	3	—
Not ready for separate state	2	4	1	—
WHY FAVOR				
Whites hate us, always will	5	5	5	4
NOT SURE	15	10	19	13

CHAPTER 8

QUESTION 36e

NEGROES ASSESS WHY SOME WHITES WANT TO KEEP NEGROES DOWN

	Total Rank and File %	Total Non-South %	Total South %	Leaders %
Afraid of Negroes getting ahead of them	12	12	12	—
Feel Negroes inferior	11	12	10	8
Lower class, poor white trash	11	8	13	12
Fear economic competition	10	10	10	30
Want somebody to do their work	10	7	13	7
Against Negro, want to keep him down	9	8	9	1
Prejudice, hatred	9	11	7	10
Ignorant, illiterate	9	10	8	11
Need to feel superior	8	9	7	31
Afraid	6	7	5	20
Don't want intermarriage	6	7	6	4
Tradition	6	3	8	8
Want to protect white women from Negro men	4	4	4	3
Economic reason	3	2	3	18
Afraid of Negro taking over country	3	3	2	—
Brought up that way	3	4	2	11
Want all the good things themselves	2	2	2	2
Not Christian	1	—	2	—
Older people, older generation	1	*	1	—
Not sure	12	12	12	1

* Less than 1 per cent.

QUESTION 36f

NEGROES ASSESS WHY SOME WHITES WANT TO SEE NEGROES GET AHEAD

	Total Rank and File %	Total Non-South %	Total South %	Leaders %
Feel Negroes are human too, no different	19	20	18	16
They are Christians	12	8	15	19
Want equal rights for Negroes	11	13	10	13
Want to do right thing	8	9	8	34
More intelligent, educated	7	8	7	11
Upper classes, wealthy, secure	6	5	8	7
Good people, nice	6	6	6	4
For good name of America	4	5	4	10
Feel sorry for Negro	3	3	4	4
Guilty conscience	2	2	3	5
Unprejudiced	2	3	2	—
They like the Negro	2	1	2	—
Have more contact, understand better	2	3	1	4
Something in it for them—selfish	2	2	2	3
Have a conscience—human	2	3	2	7
Brought up that way	1	1	1	4
Younger, young generation	1	1	1	—
Healthy attitude	1	2	1	2
Not sure	15	13	17	3

QUESTION 36c

ASSESSMENT OF NORTHERN WHITE ATTITUDES TOWARD NEGROES AS COMPARED TO SOUTHERN

	Total Rank and File %	Non-South %	South %	Leaders %
Northern whites better	38	36	39	49
No real difference	47	53	42	49
Not sure	15	11	19	2

QUESTION 36d

WHY NORTHERN WHITES BETTER TO NEGROES THAN SOUTHERN WHITES OR WHY NOT MUCH DIFFERENCE

	Total Rank and File %	Non-South %	South %	Leaders %
WHY NORTH BETTER				
North less prejudiced	12	14	11	25
Negroes better treated in North	7	7	7	1
Northerners help Negroes more	6	4	7	10
Negroes get better jobs in North	6	3	8	3
More contact with Negroes, understand more	2	2	3	8
WHY NO DIFFERENCE				
Attitudes same, laws different	12	12	12	15
Whites are whites	8	8	8	2
White Southerners more honest about prejudice	6	10	3	5
All whites against Negroes	4	6	3	1
North not completely integrated	3	3	3	2
Not all Southerners against Negroes	2	4	1	2
There are Southerners in North, Northerners in South	2	1	2	—
Depends on individual, not area	2	2	1	3
All concerned about our problems	1	1	1	1
NOT SURE	27	23	30	22

QUESTION 36m

ATTITUDE TOWARD WHITE MODERATES

	Total Rank and File %	Total Non-South %	Total South %	Leaders %
More helpful	29	29	30	46
More harmful	31	32	30	40
Not sure	40	39	40	14

QUESTION 36n

REASONS FOR ATTITUDE TOWARD WHITE MODERATES

	Total Rank and File %
WHY HELPFUL	
All help welcome	13
For equal rights too	5
At least positive	3
Against KKK	3
Keep civil-rights drive under control	3
Help persuade diehard segregationists	3
WHY HARMFUL	
Too slow	14
Weak, indecisive	6
NOT SURE	50

QUESTION 36h

WHY WHITE ATTITUDES ARE BETTER, WORSE OR UNCHANGED COMPARED TO FIVE YEARS AGO

	Total Rank and File %	Non-South %	South %	Leaders %
BETTER				
Because of Negro pressure	12	13	13	24
Negroes are better off now	9	9	10	8
More whites aware—public attention	5	7	3	37
More realize Negroes deserve equal rights	5	5	5	12
Negroes getting better jobs	4	4	4	1
Less discrimination on buses and in restaurants	4	3	4	3
Better schools	3	2	3	—
More contact with Negroes, learning about them	3	3	3	4
Government backing Negro now	3	2	4	9
Less prejudice	1	1	1	—
Whites speaking up more	1	1	1	2
New generation alive and aware	1	1	1	—
Better in North and West	1	—	1	—
WORSE				
Negro pressure and demonstration caused resentment	2	2	2	3
UNCHANGED				
Still fighting Negro demands	13	15	12	3
Don't talk or act differently	3	1	5	1
Negroes no better off	3	3	3	—
Can't end prejudice in five years	3	3	3	—
NOT SURE	24	25	22	8

QUESTION 35a

ASSESSMENT OF WHITE INSTITUTIONS IN STRUGGLE FOR NEGRO RIGHTS

	Total Rank and File %	Non-South %	South %	Leaders %
KENNEDY ADMINISTRATION				
More helpful	88	82	85	95
More harmful	2	3	1	4
Not sure	10	15	14	1
U.S. SUPREME COURT				
More helpful	85	79	81	94
More harmful	2	2	1	2
Not sure	13	19	18	4
CATHOLIC PRIESTS				
More helpful	58	54	57	74
More harmful	5	8	3	9
Not sure	37	38	40	17
CONGRESS				
More helpful	54	51	56	31
More harmful	9	13	7	40
Not sure	37	36	37	29
JEWS				
More helpful	44	49	37	73
More harmful	9	10	7	8
Not sure	47	41	56	19
LABOR UNIONS				
More helpful	40	41	36	54
More harmful	26	31	20	28
Not sure	34	28	44	18
WHITE CHURCHES				
More helpful	24	29	19	36
More harmful	24	25	21	41
Not sure	52	46	60	23
BUS COMPANIES				
More helpful	39	36	40	14
More harmful	22	26	21	48
Not sure	39	38	39	38
STATE GOVERNMENT				
More helpful	35	41	27	34
More harmful	32	23	36	39
Not sure	33	36	37	27

ASSESSMENT OF WHITE INSTITUTIONS IN STRUGGLE FOR NEGRO RIGHTS (*Cont.*)

	Total Rank and File %	Non-South %	South %	Leaders %
LOCAL AUTHORITIES				
More helpful	30	33	24	38
More harmful	35	25	39	45
Not sure	35	42	37	17
MOVIE THEATERS				
More helpful	20	25	14	16
More harmful	38	33	40	49
Not sure	42	42	46	35
GENERAL BUSINESSES				
More helpful	19	20	17	14
More harmful	39	39	36	62
Not sure	42	41	47	24
HOTELS AND MOTELS				
More helpful	16	17	13	19
More harmful	43	43	40	47
Not sure	36	40	47	34
REAL-ESTATE COMPANIES				
More helpful	16	14	16	4
More harmful	48	55	36	87
Not sure	36	31	48	9
PUERTO RICANS				
More helpful	10	14	6	20
More harmful	15	19	12	11
Not sure	75	67	82	69

QUESTIONS 35b, c

WHITE INSTITUTIONS CONSIDERED MOST HELPFUL AND MOST HARMFUL TO NEGRO RIGHTS

| | MOST HELPFUL | | | | MOST HARMFUL | | | |
	Total Rank and File %	Non-South %	South %	Leaders %	Total Rank and File %	Non-South %	South %	Leaders %
Kennedy Administration	50	50	51	25	1	1	1	—
U.S. Supreme Court	32	32	32	70	1	1	2	1
Congress	13	13	13	1	2	2	2	12
Catholic priests	9	11	8	2	1	2	*	—
Labor unions	9	11	8	1	11	13	10	8
White churches	5	7	4	—	8	9	8	9
Jews	5	7	4	9	2	3	1	—
Local authorities	5	7	3	1	14	8	20	12
State government	4	7	2	1	14	9	18	9
Bus companies	3	5	3	—	5	6	4	2
Movie theaters	2	3	1	—	8	10	7	3
Real-estate companies	2	2	3	3	15	26	7	38
Hotels/motels	1	2	1	1	9	10	—	2
Puerto Ricans	1	1	1	—	6	9	4	—
Not sure	4	2	6	—	24	20	28	18

* Less than 1 per cent.

QUESTION 36i

NEGROES ASSESS WHITE ATTITUDES ON NEGRO RIGHTS FIVE YEARS FROM NOW

	Total Rank and File %	Non-South %	South %	Leaders %
Better attitude	73	73	74	93
Worse attitude	2	1	2	—
Stay same	11	11	10	4
Not sure	14	15	14	3

QUESTION 36j

WHY WHITE ATTITUDES WILL BE BETTER OR WORSE FIVE YEARS FROM NOW

	Total Rank and File %	Non-South %	South %	Leaders %
BETTER				
Will improve	17	15	19	23
More contact with Negro will help	12	11	13	11
Pressure will do it	11	11	10	13
Will learn to accept Negro in time	8	9	8	7
Negroes getting better break now	5	4	6	1
Realizing Negro deserves better break	4	4	4	16
Support of laws and courts	4	5	4	11
Negro himself will improve and gain responsibility	3	3	4	7
More Negroes fighting now, pressures growing	3	5	3	1
Younger, new generation more openminded	2	1	2	2
Demonstrations have an effect	2	2	1	2
World pressure will create change	2	2	1	8
Support of President and government	1	2	1	—
WORSE				
Whites will always be against Negroes	3	3	4	—
Takes time, can't do it in five years	2	3	1	2
NOT SURE	21	21	21	10

CHAPTER 10

QUESTION 3d

NEGRO PREFERENCE TO WORK FOR COMPANY RUN BY WHITE MAN OR NEGRO

	Total Rank and File %	Total Non-South %	Total South %
White	5	7	5
Negro	10	7	12
No difference	79	82	76
Not sure	6	4	7

QUESTION 10

NEGRO OPINION ON INTEGRATED SCHOOLS

	Total Rank and File %	Total Non-South %	Total South %
Negro children should all go with whites	70	79	62
Negro children should not go with whites	10	8	12
Not sure	20	13	26

QUESTION 11a

WILLINGNESS TO SEND CHILDREN BY BUS TO OTHER PART OF TOWN FOR INTEGRATED SCHOOLING

	Total Rank and File %	Total Non-South %	Total South %	Leaders %
Approve pick-up by bus	50	54	47	68
Too hard on children	30	28	32	19
Not sure	20	18	21	13

QUESTION 9a

ESTIMATE OF WORK NEGRO CHILDREN WOULD DO GOING TO SCHOOL WITH WHITES

	Total Rank and File %	Total Non-South %	Total South %
Better work	65	70	62
Worse work	3	1	4
About same	19	20	18
Not sure	13	9	16

QUESTION 8b

WHY PREFER TO LIVE IN NEIGHBORHOOD WITH JUST NEGROES OR BOTH RACES

	Total Rank and File %	Total Non-South %	Total South %
NEGRO			
Get along better	13	7	17
Can't get used to rival groups	5	3	6
Less tension, conflict	3	2	3
BOTH RACES			
Should mix to know each other better	16	21	13
Race makes no difference	11	14	9
Whites and Negroes equal	7	8	6
Prefer it	6	5	7
Better neighborhood	5	7	4
Brought up in mixed neighborhood	5	7	4
Mixed neighborhoods kept up better	4	3	4
Get along better	4	5	4
Get more equal rights	2	3	2
More normal	1	1	*
Quieter, cleaner	1	2	1
Nicer people, higher class	1	1	1
If work, go to school, play together, should live together	1	1	1
NOT SURE	16	14	18

* Less than 1 per cent.

QUESTION 1c

NEGROES ASSESS WHERE THEY WILL BE FIVE YEARS FROM NOW

	Total Rank and File %	Non-South %	South %	Leaders %
PAY				
Better off	67	65	68	81
Worse off	2	2	2	7
About same	14	14	14	11
Not sure	17	19	16	1
WORK SITUATION				
Better off	64	61	66	76
Worse off	3	5	2	5
About same	15	17	14	10
Not sure	18	17	18	9
HOUSING ACCOMMODATIONS				
Better off	62	61	64	52
Worse off	2	3	1	4
About same	24	27	21	44
Not sure	12	9	14	—
BEING ABLE TO GET CHILDREN EDUCATED WITH WHITE CHILDREN				
Better off	58	51	66	66
Worse off	1	1	1	2
About same	21	33	11	30
Not sure	20	15	22	2
BEING ABLE TO EAT IN ANY RESTAURANT				
Better off	55	45	63	56
Worse off	1	1	1	2
About same	31	47	17	39
Not sure	13	7	19	3
BEING ABLE TO REGISTER AND VOTE				
Better off	42	25	55	15
Worse off	1	1	—	2
About same	48	68	34	81
Not sure	9	6	11	2

QUESTION 1d

WHY PAY WILL BE BETTER, WORSE OR SAME, IN FIVE YEARS

	Total Rank and File %
WHY BETTER	
Will get better paying job	16
Will get promoted	12
Will get raises in pay	10
More FEPCs, legislation	8
Will be better trained, educated	6
WHY WORSE OR SAME	
Will be on Social Security, welfare	6
Prices and taxes will go up	5
Discrimination will still be there	3
Won't be working then	3
NOT SURE	31

QUESTION 1d

WHY WORK SITUATION WILL BE BETTER, WORSE OR SAME, IN FIVE YEARS

	Total Rank and File %
WHY BETTER	
Discrimination in jobs will decline	17
Will be wider choice of jobs	10
Moving ahead as a race	9
More training and education	4
Government will help more	3
Wages will be better	3
NAACP and other groups will demand change	2
WHY SAME OR WORSE	
Will not be working, retired, disabled	19
Personal health will be better	2
Will be fewer jobs	2
NOT SURE	29

QUESTION 1d

WHY HOUSING ACCOMMODATIONS WILL BE BETTER, WORSE OR SAME, IN FIVE YEARS

	Total Rank and File %
WHY BETTER	
Will be less discrimination	13
Will move to a better place	10
Urban renewal will bring better housing	10
Legislation will make better	8
Will own our home	6
Will be remodeling, decorating, repairing	4
With more pay, will be able to afford better housing	2
WHY WORSE OR SAME	
Will be in same home anyway	18
Discrimination will still be here	3
Won't be able to afford, no money	1
Will still be prejudice in housing	1
NOT SURE	24

QUESTION 1d

WHY CHANCES FOR EDUCATION WITH WHITES WILL BE BETTER, WORSE OR SAME, IN FIVE YEARS

	Total Rank and File %
WHY BETTER	
More Negro children will be going to school with whites	44
Our demands will succeed	6
Government intervention will help	2
WHY WORSE	
Still will be segregation	1
WHY SAME	
Will have no children in school	11
No change	7
Have it now	5
Want segregated schools	1
NOT SURE	23

QUESTION 1d

WHY CHANCE TO EAT IN ANY RESTAURANT WILL BE BETTER, WORSE OR SAME, IN FIVE YEARS

	Total Rank and File %
WHY BETTER	
More restaurants will open up, time will do it	47
Sit-ins will make it better	2
Laws will make it better	2
Owners will want the business	2
WHY WORSE	
Still will be able to go to only certain places	2
South will stay bad, North will improve	2
WHY SAME	
Nothing will change, still won't able to afford	12
Will always eat at home	8
Will have no trouble as today	4
Will still avoid those that discriminate	1
NOT SURE	18

QUESTION 1d

WHY CHANCE TO VOTE WILL BE BETTER, WORSE OR SAME, IN FIVE YEARS

	Total Rank and File %
WHY BETTER	
Will be less discrimination in voting	23
We're more aware of value of voting	4
We'll be like everybody else	1
WHY WORSE	
Still won't be able to register in South	1
Won't be able to pay poll tax	1
Won't be any new legislation	1
WHY SAME	
Not interested in voting	5
Will vote as do now	40
NOT SURE	24

QUESTION 25g

WHY PROGRESS ON NEGRO RIGHTS TOO SLOW, TOO FAST, OR ABOUT RIGHT

	Total Rank and File %	Non-South %	South %	Leaders %
WHY TOO SLOW				
Have waited 100 years, too long	21	24	19	35
No progress, no rights, nothing done	18	18	18	28
Still many things Negroes can't do	7	7	7	7
Demonstrations show progress too slow	1	1	1	4
Negroes have no jobs	1	2	1	1
Southern Negroes still bad off	1	1	1	—
WHY TOO FAST				
Should take little at a time	1	1	2	—
WHY ABOUT RIGHT				
Takes time for action, adjustment	10	10	9	3
Can't move too fast, will cause bloodshed	6	7	6	2
Progress being made, will come	6	7	6	11
Negro has some rights	4	3	4	1
NOT SURE	24	19	26	8

NEGRO LEADERSHIP SAMPLE

Below is a list of the leading American Negroes who were interviewed in the *Newsweek* survey. The list includes persons nationally known for their role in the civil rights movement as well as individuals outstanding in their community or profession. In selecting them, *Newsweek* consulted Negroes themselves among other advisers. A certain number were unreachable or refused to be interviewed. The list does not total 100 names because two of the leaders interviewed did not want to be identified here.

REV. RALPH ABERNATHY *minister and SCLC Treasurer, Atlanta, Ga.*
T. M. ALEXANDER *businessman, Atlanta, Ga.*
HORACE C. ANDERSON *engineer, Palo Alto, Calif.*
JAMES BALDWIN *author, New York, N.Y.*
CLAUDE A. BARNETT *Director of the Associated Negro Press, Chicago, Ill.*
MRS. RUTH M. BATSON *social worker, Boston, Mass.*

GEORGE BEAVERS *insurance executive, Los Angeles, Calif.*

EDWIN C. BERRY *Chicago Director of the National Urban League, Chicago, Ill.*

REV. JAMES L. BEVEL *Field Secretary for SCLC, Cleveland, Miss.*

M. LEO BOHANON *social welfare executive, St. Louis, Mo.*

H. JULIAN BOND *Communications Director of SNCC, Atlanta, Ga.*

THOMAS BRADLEY *attorney, Executive Director of Council for United Civil Rights Leadership, and city councilman, Los Angeles, Calif.*

DOLORES BRANCHE *social worker, Chicago, Ill.*

WILEY A. BRANTON *attorney and director of voter education project, Atlanta, Ga.*

EDWARD W. BROOKE *Attorney General of Massachusetts*

REV. H. H. BROOKINS *minister, Los Angeles, Calif.*

GWENDOLYN BROOKS *poet, Chicago, Ill.*

BASIL W. BROWN *Senator, Michigan State Senate, Detroit, Mich.*

WILLIE L. BROWN, JR. *attorney and NAACP board member, San Francisco, Calif.*

ERNEST CALLOWAY *Associate Research Director of the Central Conference of Teamsters, St. Louis, Mo.*

KENNETH E. CAMPBELL *alderman, 20th Ward, Chicago, Ill.*

DAVID CARLISLE *engineering executive in space research and development, Los Angeles, Calif.*

A. M. CARTER *businessman, Atlanta, Ga.*

YOLANDE H. CHAMBERS *businessman, Detroit, Mich.*

DR. KENNETH CLARK *professor of psychology, College of the City of New York*

WILLIAM L. CLAY *alderman, 26th Ward, St. Louis, Mo.*

REV. ALBERT B. CLEAGE, JR. *minister, Detroit, Mich.*

WARREN R. COCHRANE *Executive Secretary of Georgia Association of Democratic Clubs and a general secretary of YMCA, Atlanta, Ga.*

FRANK COLLIER *reporter for Reuters, Oakland, Calif.*

WILLIAM B. COLLIER, JR. *real-estate broker, Chicago, Ill.*

DR. DANIEL A. COLLINS *dentist, Mill Valley, Calif.*

MRS. OLIVER CRAWFORD *society and community affairs leader, Chicago, Ill.*

SAMMY DAVIS, JR. *entertainer, Los Angeles, Calif.*

HOLMES (DADDY-O) DAYLIE *disk jockey, Chicago, Ill.*

LLOYD DICKENS *assemblyman and Harlem District Leader, New York, N.Y.*

EDWARD DUDLEY *Manhattan Borough President, New York, N.Y.*

JOHN DUNCAN *District Commissioner, Washington, D.C.*

REV. JOSEPH H. EVANS *minister, Chicago, Ill.*

JOSEPH A. FAISON *insurance executive, Philadelphia, Pa.*

JAMES L. FARMER *National Director of CORE, New York, N.Y.*

REV. WALTER FAUNTROY *minister and SCLC representative, Washington, D.C.*

ARTHUR Q. FUNN *attorney and National Urban League counsel, New York, N.Y.*

DICK GREGORY *entertainer and NAACP board member, Chicago, Ill.*

MRS. GRACE T. HAMILTON *executive committeewoman of the Southern Regional Council, Atlanta, Ga.*

GLADYS HARRINGTON *social worker, former chairman of N.Y. CORE, New York, N.Y.*

GEORGE S. HARRIS *insurance company president, Chicago, Ill.*

AARON HENRY *pharmacist, write-in candidate for Governor in 1963, board member of SCLC, state conference president of NAACP, Clarksdale, Miss.*

REV. R. A. HILDEBRAND *minister and NAACP director, New York, N.Y.*

DONALD HOLLOWELL *attorney, Atlanta, Ga.*

MRS. RUBY HURLEY *Southeastern Regional Director of NAACP, Atlanta, Ga.*

REV. E. F. JACKSON *minister and NAACP leader, Washington, D.C.*

REV. E. W. JARRETT *minister, Gadsden, Ala.*

HON. BERNARD JEFFERSON *appellate judge, Los Angeles, Calif.*

MRS. EMILY JOHNSON *president of a real-estate firm, Los Angeles, Calif.*

JOHN H. JOHNSON *President, Johnson Publishing Co., Inc. (Jet, Ebony, etc.), Chicago, Ill.*

DR. JACK KIMBROUGH *dentist, San Diego, Calif.*

MRS. JEWEL LA FONTANT *attorney, Chicago, Ill.*

WESTLEY W. LAW *board member and state conference president of the NAACP, Savannah, Ga.*

DR. T. K. LAWLESS *dermatologist, Chicago, Ill.*

LOUIS LOMAX *author and NAACP board member, New York, N.Y.*

MALCOLM X *Black Muslim leader and preacher, New York, N.Y.*

DR. BENJAMIN E. MAYS *President of Morehouse College, Atlanta, Ga.*

HAROLD L. MILES *police captain, Chicago, Ill.*

BILLIE MILLS *councilman, Los Angeles, Calif.*

MRS. DELLA MITCHELL *CORE chairman, High Point, N.C.*

NATALIE HINDERAS MONAGAS *concert pianist and teacher, Philadelphia, Pa.*

CECIL B. MOORE *attorney and president of Philadelphia branch of NAACP*

FRED H. MOORE *attorney, Charleston, S.C.*

REV. H. RANDOLPH MOORE *minister, Los Angeles, Calif.*

ALLAN MORRISON *chief of N.Y. bureau, Johnson Publishing Co., Inc.*

DR. JAMES M. NABRIT, JR. *President of Howard University, Washington, D.C.*

JESSE OWENS *former track star and now businessman, Chicago, Ill.*

JAMES V. PASCHAL *restaurant owner, Atlanta, Ga.*

MATTHEW J. PERRY *attorney, Columbia, S.C.*

CECIL F. POOLE *U.S. Attorney for Northern District of California, San Francisco, Calif.*

LINCOLN G. POPE, JR. *Representative, Massachusetts House of Representatives, Boston, Mass.*

JACKIE ROBINSON *former baseball star, now businessman and President of United Church Men, New York, N.Y.*

HARVEY N. SCHMIDT *attorney, Philadelphia, Pa.*

GEORGE SCHUYLER *associate editor for* The Pittsburgh Courier *in New York, N.Y.*

CORNELIUS SCOTT *editor* The Atlanta World, *Atlanta, Ga.*

REV. MARSHALL L. SHEPARD *minister and Philadelphia councilman*

REV. ROBERT L. T. SMITH *minister, Congressional candidate in November 1963, Jackson, Miss.*

MRS. MURIEL SNOWDEN *associate director of Freedom House, Boston, Mass.*

HON. VAINO SPENCER *municipal judge, Los Angeles, Calif.*

REV. A. K. STANLEY *minister, Greensboro, N.C.*

CHESTER E. STOVALL *director, Department of Welfare, St. Louis, Mo.*

DEMPSEY J. TRAVIS *banker, Chicago, Ill.*

WILLIS F. WARD *attorney, Detroit, Mich.*

DR. CLINTON E. WARNER *physician, Atlanta, Ga.*

MRS. BENNETTA WASHINGTON *high school principal, Washington, D.C.*

JAMES L. WATSON *judge of New York County Civil Court, former State Senator, New York, N.Y.*

REV. S. LEON WHITNEY *minister, Jackson, Miss.*

ROY WILKINS *Executive Secretary of the NAACP, New York, N.Y.*

HOWARD B. WOODS *executive editor of the* St. Louis Argus, *St. Louis, Mo.*

ABE WOODSON *defensive halfback for the San Francisco 49ers, San Francisco, Calif.*

C. R. YATES *businessman, Atlanta, Ga.*

WHITNEY YOUNG, JR. *Executive Director of the National Urban League, New York, N.Y.*

INDEX TO NEGRO PERSONAGES
AND ORGANIZATIONS

ABOUT THE AUTHORS

WILLIAM J. BRINK, who was born in Indianapolis and graduated from Indiana University, has been a journalist for more than fifteen years. He was with United Press International before coming to *Newsweek* in 1956. As a general editor of that magazine, he wrote a number of stories on the civil rights movement. In 1961, he became chief of the *Newsweek* bureau in Chicago and two years later Business Editor of *Newsweek*. Mr. Brink is married and has four children.

LOUIS HARRIS is president of the marketing and public-opinion research firm bearing his name. This firm conducted the surveys described in the present volume, as well as the monthly, topical *Newsweek* poll. Before stepping out of the field of private political surveys, the firm did research in 214 election campaigns on all levels of government; it continues to do research for major companies. Mr. Harris was a faculty associate at Columbia University for ten years. In 1954, he published a book, *Is There a Republican Majority?* (Harper & Row). He recently became a CBS news consultant and writes a weekly newspaper column syndicated through the Washington *Post*. A native of New Haven, Conn., Mr. Harris was graduated from the University of North Carolina. He has a wife and three children.